Free Methodist Handbook: Marriage and Weddings

Dr. John Wesley Slider

Copyright © 2011, 2020 John Wesley Slider

All rights reserved.

ISBN-10: 1460939565
ISBN-13: 978-1460939567

DEDICATION

This book is dedicated to Lillian, my wife of more than forty years.

CONTENTS

	Introduction	i
1	An Overview of Marriage in the Bible	1
2	Genesis 2.21-24 – Reuniting the One	15
3	Genesis 2.25; 3.7-10, 16 – The Fallen State	21
4	The Wisdom of Jesus Ben Sirach 9.1-9 – A List of Don'ts	25
5	Jesus' Teachings on Divorce from Matthew, Mark, and Luke	33
6	1 Corinthians 11.2-6 – Men and Women in the Community of Faith	47
7	Ephesians 5.21-33 – The Mystery Is Great	55
8	Weddings and Marriage in the Free Methodist Church	61
9	Practices and Guidelines for Weddings in the Church	69
10	Marriage Counseling and Important Issues to Address	79
11	The Solemnization of Matrimony – The Free Methodist Church	91
12	A Service of Marriage from the Methodist Church	97
13	A Ritual for the Reaffirmation of the Marriage Covenant	105
14	A Service for the Blessing of a Civil Marriage	109
	About the Author	115

INTRODUCTION

One of the more enjoyable pastoral activities is joining a man and a woman in marriage. Pastors should be good stewards of their ordination and office in performing weddings. Pastors need to find a comfortable balance between being too restrictive and too open in performing weddings.

In the Free Methodist tradition, marriage is taken very seriously, and weddings should not be performed for just any couple. Yet, the counseling and wedding provide an excellent opportunity to proclaim the love of God in Christ and establish a pastoral relationship with persons who would not in other situations have the opportunity to hear the good news or get to know a Christian pastor.

I wrote this book with three objectives. I want to provide a framework for pastors — including myself — to use in pre-marital counseling. I also wanted to have a resource to give couples in planning their weddings and to use throughout their marriage. I also wanted to have a book to use for study groups within the congregation. For me this book fills all three objectives.

My approach to this book has been rather serious, and hopefully academic. The foundation for it has been my thirty-two years as a United Methodist pastor (1979-2010), and now (since 2010) as a Free Methodist pastor. I have appreciated both traditions and their influences on my Wesleyan-Methodist perspective. I am particularly enjoying learning the more evangelistic perspective of my new denomination. I have drawn on both streams of the Wesleyan-Methodist movement for liturgy.

I should also mention that the scripture passages are my own translations. I mention this only to give the reader a warning.

I hope this book will provide some assistance to other Free Methodist pastors and churches. May God bless you.

John Wesley Slider
Saint Matthews, Kentucky
February 2011

FREE METHODIST HANDBOOK: MARRIAGE AND WEDDINGS

1 AN OVERVIEW OF MARRIAGE IN THE BIBLE

The Bible story spans many centuries and many cultures. Regardless of this broad span of history and social development, the Bible gives a relatively consistent view of marriage. Marriage was a universal practice and an important part of the ancient Middle Eastern cultures found in the Old and New Testaments.

Biblical marriage is personal, spiritual, and sexual companionship between a man and a woman. The purpose of marriage in the Bible was to provide children, to preserve the family lines, and to contain sexual passions. Marriage was viewed as a covenant or alliance between two families.

The Bible sees marriage as being ordained by God for the good of His people. Proverbs 12.8 says that for a man, the good life consists of faith, home, children, and a good wife. Proverbs 5.19 urges that love be a part of marriage, and Ecclesiastes encourages a man to enjoy life with the love of one woman.

As we look at marriage in the Bible we should be aware of two pitfalls. One pitfall is that we assume that there is only one type of marriage found in the Bible. There were many types of marriage in the Bible and many marriages. Not all marriages and types of marriage were healthy. For example, in the bigamous marriages of Jacob to his wives, Leah and Rachel, and his relationships with his concubines, Zilpah and Bilhah, we find tense familial relationships, to say the least.

The second pitfall we should avoid is to assume that we can transplant a Biblical blueprint into our contemporary American culture. The Bible assumes a Middle Eastern culture that was patriarchal. Still, it is from the Bible that our culture has received the basic principles of equal value of all persons before God and in marriage. In examining the Bible for an understanding of marriage we should, therefore, not look for a blueprint, but for guiding principles through which God will bless our marriages.

The Bible is a story of the human and divine interaction. It is not primarily a code or list of platitudes. In the Bible we can find ourselves – who we are and who we should be – in relation to God. The Bible is the story of a dynamic relationship from the human perspective. In this way we can see that the Biblical view of marriage does not hold for us a checklist that leads to marital bliss. The Bible contains the story God's offer of abundant life – of which marriage is a part – and the efforts of persons to respond to that offer by faith within the context of their world.

Limitations on Marriage in the Bible

The Bible places certain limitations on who a person can marry. These limitations are both endogamous (within a defined circle) and exogamous (outside a defined circle).

The exogamous boundaries on marriage in the Bible limit marriage to persons outside a certain kinship circle. For example, Genesis 20.12 forbids marriage to close relations on the mother's side. Leviticus 18 and 20 exclude the marriage (or sexual relations) of a man with his mother's sister, father's sister, father's brother's wife, and brother's wife. The Bible forbids incestuous relations (and thereby marriage) by a man with his mother, stepmother, sister, granddaughter, stepsister, aunt, daughter-in-law, sister-in-law, and mother-in-law.

There were outer (endogamous) boundaries for marriage in the Bible, also. These outer limitations essentially exclude marriage outside the ethnic or religious group. These limitations were sometimes ignored (for example, Samson rejected endogamy in Judges 14.3). Endogamous limitations were often violently enforced.

Exogamy and endogamy appear in the Bible because the people of the Bible recognized the social and theological dangers that were posed by marriage beyond either of these limits. Violation of the exogamous prohibitions would threaten other relationships within the family and pose some biological threats to the community as well. The family relationships (father, mother, brother, sister, aunt, uncle, and even relatives by marriage) are of greater theological and social value than the opportunity to marry or have sexual relations with a close family member.

We readily accept the exogamous boundaries of our culture which are Biblically based, but these boundaries were not always universally accepted by the greater culture which surrounded the people of the Bible — especially in the Old Testament. Our culture endorses these prohibitions and finds them endorsed by contemporary psychology, sociology, biology, and ethics.

We tend to question the endogamous boundaries on marriage in the Bible because they appear to us to be racially motivated. We tend to forget that religion and race were closely linked in the Old Testament. Marriage outside the ethnic community threatened to undermine (and often did undermine) the faith of the community. The emphasis, then, was not racial purity, but religious purity.

In the New Testament there were no prohibitions on marriage between persons of different races. Paul, however, prohibited marriage with unbelievers by the members of the church at Corinth (2 Corinthians 6.14-15). Paul's concern, especially at Corinth, was the pressures that threatened the faithfulness of the Corinthian Christians from inside and outside the church and those pressures included marriage to persons outside the faith.

Should we follow Paul's prohibition on marriage outside the Christian faith? Certainly we can see the value of sharing a set of core values and beliefs with a spouse. The real question should be: How much a part of my life is my faith in Jesus Christ? If your faith in Christ is central to who you are as a person, you probably will not find lasting happiness with a person that does not share that faith unless you compromise your faith. Paul would suggest that such a compromise is not only unwise, but it gains nothing in the end.

Arranging Marriages

The normative practice in the Old Testament was for the father to initiate a marriage including the selection of the bride for his son (for example, Genesis 24.4 and 34.8). Sometimes a father would give his daughter for marriage to his prospective son-in-law as in Genesis 29.28, Joshua 15.16-17, and Judges 1.12-13. The father's role, of course, did not rule out the mother's involvement or the presence of love in the marriage. In exceptional instances the mother would arrange a marriage for her son (e.g., Genesis 21.21). There are also several occasions where a man takes for himself a wife (Genesis 4.19, 6.2, 11.29, etc.).

We cannot help but notice in the Old Testament that wives were treated much like property in arranging marriages. There are examples of purchasing wives (Genesis 31.15, 34.12, Exodus 22.17, etc.) or service in exchange for a wife (Genesis 29.20-28). Though Jeremiah 6.12 lists wives as a part of the property taken in battle, evidence of marriage by capture of a female during war is not very solid in the Old Testament.

In the primitive societies reflected in the early Old Testament period, daughters were a liability and infanticide of female children was apparently a common practice. When females became scarce, they were often taken by force. That there is no solid evidence for this practice on the part of the people of God in the Old Testament suggests that they held to a higher standard in the treatment of women. Marriage by capture from other groups would have violated the endogamous limitations.

Old Testament practices show that the bride was a passive participant in the marriage transaction. The New Testament, though it does not reveal what the practices of the early Church were, does show a high regard for women. Indeed, within the Christian community there appeared to be an openness and equality between the sexes reflected in the leadership and participation of women in the church. We can safely say that Christianity moved beyond the role assigned to women in the Old Testament. Though they still had to operate within the cultural constraints of their day, men and women within the Christian community related to one another as equally as possible on the basis of their relationship with Christ.

Though families still play a subtle role in the choice of a spouse we are in the position now where there is more freedom for both partners. Still, as persons of faith as we search for a spouse we must recognize the role of the family for a marriage creates more than a new relationship between a man and a woman. In a real sense both families are united.

Who's the Boss?

The Bible presents two models of authority in a marriage. In a matriarchal marriage the authority rests in the wife/mother. In a patriarchal marriage the authority rests in the husband/father.

There is significant evidence of matriarchal marriage in the Old Testament. Indeed Genesis 2.24 suggests a matriarchal marriage with the man leaving his father and mother for his wife.

One type of matriarchal marriage found in the Old Testament occurs when the husband settles permanently in the wife's home and the children remain in the mother's control. The marriage of Moses and Zipporah (Exodus 2.21-22) suggests such an arrangement.

Another type of matriarchal marriage found in the Old Testament occurs when the husband visits the home of the wife periodically and the children remain in the control of the mother. A variation of this pattern would be for the wife to reside near the husband with her children, but to have her own quarters (Genesis 31.33, Judges 4.17-18).

Related to matriarchal marriage are the matrilineal and matronymic families. In a matrilineal family the descent of the children is traced through the mother. In a matronymic family the children's names come by and through the mother.

The patriarchal marriage, however, is the dominant form in the Bible (Genesis 36.9-42, Numbers 1.1-3.39, 26.5-62, Ruth 4.18-22, 1 Chronicles 1-9, and Ezra 2.3-61, 10.18-43). Genesis 3.16 suggests that a wife's subordination to the authority of her husband is a result of the human fall into sin and not a part of God's plan. Paul and other New Testament writers continue the patriarchal pattern (1 Corinthians 11.2-3, Ephesians 5.22-24, Colossians 3.18, and 1 Peter 3.1-7). Patrilineal and patronymic families are also the more common pattern.

In our society we tend to value the equal participation of husband and wife in the decisions of a marriage and family. Equality within a marriage, while the most healthy situation given our cultural context, is also the most difficult to maintain. Shared responsibilities and roles based on the spirit of Christ help us deal with issues of authority, power, and control in a marriage. Decisions must be made, and often times they are easier to make when only one person decides. If, however, in a marriage both partners approach one another with the same self-giving love that is in Christ, then authority, power, and control are not the focus. Rather both persons look first to the needs of the partner and the entire family.

Monogamy or Polygamy

Monogamy is the general Biblical practice for marriage. Monogamy is the most frequent form of marriage in the Old Testament and is assumed in the New Testament. The first marriage in the Bible was monogamous (Gen 2.24).

Though monogamy is the Biblical norm, there are very visible polygamous marriages found in the scriptures.

Polygyny - the marriage of a man to more than one woman at a single time – appears in the Bible, whereas polyandry – the marriage of a woman to more than one man at a single time – does not. Polygamy in the Bible is usually bigamy (two wives).

Polygamy appears to have been more widespread in ancient Israel and began to disappear as society developed. Persons entered into multiple marriages in order to produce children (Abraham in Genesis 16.3), to seal political alliances (Solomon in 1 Kings 11.1-3), for love (Jacob in Genesis 29.18), and for lust (David in 2 Samuel 11.15, 27). Primarily, though, in primitive cultures of semi-nomads and farmers, multiple marriages were used to produce male children and thereby give the family workers. The only social options available to fathers who wanted to produce more sons/laborers were either polygamy or divorce. As the semi-nomadic lifestyle decreased, the practice of polygamy decreased and monogamy became more practical.

Not all was peaceful in multiple marriages. Conflict and dissension in polygamous situations in the Bible are apparent, especially if the husband showed a preference. Indeed, the Hebrew root of the word for second wife used in the Old Testament means *show hostility*.

There is one type of multiple-person marriage in the Old Testament that is curious to us today. This marriage is the Levirate marriage. *Lever* means *husband's brother* in Hebrew. In a Levirite marriage the brother-in-law would marry his deceased brother's childless widow (Deuteronomy 25.5-10). These marriages and sexual relations are a contradiction to the prohibitions on a man having sexual relations with his sister-in-law (Leviticus 18.16, 20.21). They were needed in order to prevent marriage by the widow to someone outside the family, to continue the deceased brother/husband's name and lineage, to preserve the family's estate, and to provide for the widow's welfare in a culture whose only welfare system was the family (e.g. Ruth and Naomi). There is some suggestion that this practice continued into Jesus' day.

The New Testament shows that the early Church assumed that monogamy was the appropriate situation for marriage. The entire Bible shows a movement toward this ideal. Any other practice is in opposition to the consistent teachings of Christianity.

Betrothal

In the Bible betrothal means more than we understand it to mean. We understand betrothal to simply be an engagement of promise to marriage. In the Bible the betrothed parties were considered husband and wife (Genesis 19.14, Deuteronomy 22.23-23, 28.30, Judges 14.15, 15.1, 2 Samuel 3.14). Intercourse with a woman betrothed to another man resulted in death, but intercourse with a woman not betrothed required marriage of the man and woman (Deuteronomy 22.23-28). Betrothal could only be ended with a divorce (e.g., Joseph and Mary).

Betrothal means *paying the price.* The betrothal period was the time between paying the marriage price and the ceremony.

The marriage price or gift from the husband to the bride's father served many valuable social functions. It established the prestige and social status of the giver and husband-to-be. The marriage gift assigned value to the bride. It symbolically transferred part of the life of the husband to the bride's family, and it was a means by which the husband gave himself in exchange for the bride. Finally, it was a seal of the covenant or promise of marriage.

We continue betrothal practices today through the giving of an engagement ring, wedding gifts, and the period of engagement.

The Ceremony

The ceremony, which marked the beginning of a marriage, was an event for the entire community. The bride and groom wore special clothing, much of which sounds familiar to us – ornaments, garlands, jewelry, and a bridal veil. Both the bride and groom had special attendants for the ceremony. The ceremony was highlighted by the processions of the groom's and the bride's parties, music, and a feast. At the end of the ceremony the husband would open his robe and take his wife into himself. The couple would then be escorted to a special tent or room called the bridal chamber in which they would spend their first evening together.

Ceremony and ritual mark important events in our lives and allow us to remember a beginning. In order to have meaning, though, ceremonies must reflect who we are and what we want to say.

Sexual Relations

In the Bible sex is fundamentally good. Sex is a part of God's creative action (Genesis 2.21-24). The Biblical reasons for sexual relations are expression of love, production of children, and giving of mutual pleasure.

Intimacy and closeness are important to the true meaning of sexual relations (Genesis 4.1, 17, 25, etc.). The word for *intercourse* in the Old Testament comes from the Hebrew root *to know*.

The Bible maintains that the only appropriate form of sexual relations is between a man and a woman in the context of a marriage (1 Corinthians 7.1-4, for example). The Song of Songs portrays the passionate longing of two lovers for marriage and celebrates sexual pleasures within a marriage. Homosexual relationships (and marriages) are forbidden in the Old Testament and this ban is continued in the New Testament.

In the Bible abstinence from sexual relations is required outside of marriage. The New Testament allows for the practice of abstinence within a marriage only when both parties agree and only for a limited period. The Old Testament suggests that the celibate lifestyle was only appropriate for those unable to function sexually (Deuteronomy 23.1). In Matthew 19.12 Jesus says that there are those who choose celibacy in order to focus on the Kingdom of God.

These teachings are valid for us today. Sexual relations between a man and a woman in the context of marriage are a part of the intimacy of that union and should be encouraged. Sex in this context should not be source of guilt or shame, nor performed out of duty. Sex within a Christian marriage is an expression of the intimate love of a husband and wife and as a part of the grace of God.

Adultery

Because of the nature of marriage and the role of women in the culture reflected in the Old Testament, adultery was seen as a violation of the husband's sole possession of the wife and of his assurance that the children of his marriage were his. The Old Testament prohibitions against adultery are directed at both men and women, but mostly toward men (Exodus 20.14, Leviticus 18.20, 20.10, etc.). Malachi

2.14 carries a condemnation of a husband's faithlessness to the wife of his youth.

The Old Testament punished adultery with death. The New Testament finds adultery to be a sin which may be forgiven (John 8.2-11); but Jesus teaches that adultery is more than an action. It also occurs in our thoughts (Matthew 5.20). Remarriage after the death of a spouse was not considered adultery in the early Church (Romans 7.3).

The Biblical view of sexual relations conforms to its view of adultery. Sexual relations are appropriate only within marriage. Adultery is a violation of the physical, emotional, and spiritual intimacy of the marital relationship.

Divorce

There are examples of divorce in both the Old and New Testaments. Divorce was generally permitted on the initiative of the husband (Deuteronomy 24.1-4, Hosea 2.2, Matthew 19.8). There is some suggestion that the allowance for divorce was being abused during Jesus' day.

The general reason for divorce was that some indecency or adultery was committed (Deuteronomy 24.1). The Old Testament permitted divorce on the grounds of religious differences (Ezra 10.3), but the New Testament does not agree (1 Corinthians 7.12-15, 1 Peter 3.1-2) and encourages spouses to remain with their non-believing partners. The possibility of taking back the divorced spouse is extended in Isaiah 54.6. Marriage of a divorced person is considered adultery in Matthew 5.32, Mark 10.11-12, and Luke 16.18.

Divorce is a prevalent reality in our culture and the Church must respond to it in healing ways. Divorce should not be the standard for family life, nor should it be anything but the option of last resort. Too often divorce is seen as an easy escape from dealing with important issues in a wounded marriage.

Yet, divorce is sometimes the only option in relationships that have clearly become abusive in any way. In these cases the Church needs to seek healing for all parties, but should also seek to defend the abused person.

Divorce is a sin because fundamentally it is the destruction of a relationship – the most intimate of all human relationships – and that is what sin is. Divorce, however, is not an unforgivable sin. The sin rests in those who destroyed the intimate relationship and in those who fail to bring healing before, during, and after the divorce.

This chapter has given a quick overview of marriage in the Bible. The next several chapters will examine several scriptures in detail in order to give some depth to the discussion of marriage.

NOTES

John Wesley Slider

2 GENESIS 2.21-24 - REUNITING THE ONE

Then God Yahweh cast a deep sleep upon the man (Adam) and, when he was asleep, He took one of his ribs and closed up the flesh at that spot. And God Yahweh fashioned into a woman ('Issa) the rib that He had removed from the man (Adam), and He brought her to the man (Adam). The man (Adam) said: "This at last is bone of my bone and flesh of my flesh. She shall be called woman ('Issa) for she was taken from man ('Ish).

Thus it is that man ('Ish) leaves his father and mother and clings to his wife, and they become one flesh.

This first passage about marriage comes from a source that most scholars date in its current form from around the tenth century BC or about 1,000 years before Christ and approximately 3,000 years ago. This well-known passage is a part of the story of God's creative activity.

Reuniting Adam

As the translation displays there are two words for *Man* used. The Hebrew word *adam* (man or mankind) is based on the root *ADM* and is closely related to *adama* (soil, earth). Adam can be understood to mean *created man or being*. It is Adam who is created in the image of God.

It is this Adam who is separated by God to create male (*Ish*) and female (*Issa*). We should not draw too much from this examination of the words, however. *Ish* and *Issa* appear to be related in the transliteration from Hebrew to English, but they are probably not to be closely connected. In addition, though verses 21-22 say that from Adam woman is formed; verse 23 suggests that from *Ish* comes *Issa*. The word for *rib* can also mean *side*. Still the basic idea remains. The original unity of the created being is separated into two parts.

The two parts of the whole are reunited. This reuniting of the created being suggests that the relationship between husband and wife is more than a social institution. It is part of the re-establishment of the wholeness of a human being. Man is incomplete without a permanent and intimate relationship (emotional, spiritual, and physical) with Woman. The same holds true for Woman.

Creating a Family *Ex Nihil*

The scripture says the man leaves his parents and clings to his wife. This action reflects leaving the old for the new. A new family is created where none existed before.

This model for marriage is both monogamous and matriarchal. This "first" marriage is between one man and one woman only. It is the man who leaves his parents and joins with the woman – even clings to her. A permanent relationship is established through marriage.

Single Persons

Does this mean that single persons are incomplete? Not necessarily. It does mean that single persons need to seek their completion and fulfillment outside of marriage, but as with married persons, within the context of the grace of God. Jesus suggests that there are those who are blessed with the gift of singleness and celibacy in order to better comprehend and participate in the Kingdom of God. The single person, as we all do, depends upon God for his or her wholeness in life. This blessing is not for everyone, and even though John Wesley would call singleness the "more excellent way." He eventually married.

God's Role

God has an active role in the reuniting of the two into one. Verse 22 says that it is God who brought the woman to the man. It is God who makes the introduction. God initiates the reuniting. The relationship between a man and a woman is a part of God's creative activity. Marriages in which God does not play an active part will not be situations in which either partner will be brought into wholeness.

Divorce

This passage has implications for our view of divorce. In a marriage in which God has been actively at work creating wholeness, divorce tears apart what God has created. In a marriage without the presence and involvement of God, divorce is simply an admission of reality – there was not a relationship of intimacy, which brought wholeness and completeness to both persons.

Homosexuality

This scripture rules out homosexual relationships. The wholeness cannot be given in a relationship between two of the same parts. Wholeness comes only with the reunion of the complimentary parts of Creation.

In the marriage of a man and a woman God reunites the two into one. Both are blessed with wholeness of life. God creates this relationship out of nothing, blessing the man and the woman by His love.

NOTES

John Wesley Slider

3 GENESIS 2.25; 3.7-10, 16 - THE FALLEN STATE

The two of them were naked, the man and his wife, yet they felt no shame.

Then the eyes of both were opened and they discovered that they were naked; so they sewed fig leaves together and made themselves loincloths. They heard the sound of God Yahweh as He was walking in the garden at the breezy time of day; and the man and his wife hid from God Yahweh among the trees of the garden.

God Yahweh called to the man and said to him, "Where are you?"

He answered, "I heard the sound of You in the garden; but I was afraid because I was naked, so I hid."

To the woman He (God) said, "I will make your pangs intense in childbearing. In pain shall you bear children; yet your urge shall be for your husband, and he shall be your master."[1]

---

[1]Author's Note: The reader will forgive me for jumping from verse to verse. I have only reproduced the salient verses in the story of the fall of humanity.

Verses 2.25 and 3.8 give us a glimpse of life as God would have it for us – life in paradise. We find an intimate relationship between the man and woman. We see them both naked – completely open to one another – without shame. God is included in this intimacy. The marriage involves three – Man, Woman, and God.

The Results of Sin

The sin of the Man and the Woman is that they break their intimate relationship with God – the third party in the marriage. They abuse their freedom that God has given them to go beyond their created boundaries and become "like God." Separation from God occurs in the disobedience of the Man and the Woman.

As a result of the Sin, not only is the intimacy broken with God but also it is broken between the Man and the Woman. They do not become like God; they become less than human. Once they were reunited, now they are separated.

In the fallen state fear and shame replace intimacy with both God and the partner. Power dominates the relationship between the Man and the Woman. The Woman relates to the Man as dependent. The Man exercises power as master.

The Hebrew writers in part used this story to explain the reality that they saw in their world. This world is one which they viewed as fallen or corrupted. It is a world which human sin has separated Creation from the Creator's intent. Relationships are separated from this intention as well.

What Does God Want for Us?

The important question arises for us: What does God want for us? Specifically, in our marriages does God want us to relate to one another and to Him in accordance with the sinful world or in accordance with His creative intention?

Certainly we cannot ignore the fact that we live in this fallen world. No matter how holy we wish to live, our holiness will be lived in the context of a sinful world.

Yet we are called to be in the world for the world's sake, not to be of the world. A part of our witness to the world is our difference from the world. It is my contention, therefore, that our model for marriage is not the world's model that is a result of sin. Marriages that follow this model are based on power and dependency, and characterized by a lack of true intimacy (physical, emotional, and spiritual), by hidden-ness and fear, and by the absence of the Creator.

Our model for marriage is God's creative intention. God seeks marriages of complete intimacy for us. These marriages link a man, a woman, and God and are expressions of the reuniting of the wholeness of creation and the wholeness of life in God's love.

NOTES

John Wesley Slider

4 THE WISDOM OF JESUS BEN SIRACH 9.1-9 -A LIST OF DO NOTS

Do not be jealous of the wife with whom you are so close, or you will show her by your bad example how she should act toward you.

Do not give a woman your heart, or she will walk all over your life.

Do not go to a prostitute because you might fall into her trap without realizing it.

Do not keep company with a singer because you might be captured by her attempts to seduce you.

Do not stare at a virgin, so that you will not be shamed by the scandal she will rightfully cause you.

Do not give a whore your heart, so you will not lose God's blessing.

Do not admire the sights in the city streets, and do not wander alone into the back alleys.

Keep your eyes off of a beautiful woman, and do not stare at the beauty, which belongs to another. The beauty of a woman has fooled many. Love has often been sparked by a glance.

Do not cuddle with another man's wife, and do not buy her drinks. If you do your hearts will grow close and you will be destroyed by your desires.

The Free Methodist Church and most Protestant denominations do not recognize the Wisdom of Jesus Ben Sirach (also known as Ecclesiasticus) as scripture. It is a part of a body of Jewish literature known as the Apocrypha. The Apocrypha consists of Jewish religious writings, which were not accepted into the list of Jewish scriptures by the rabbis.

Ecclesiasticus was written in Jerusalem about 300 BC. It is a collection of proverbs or wisdom sayings concerning how to live the good life.

These verses are included here because they would have been a part of the body of literature familiar both the Jesus and the early Church. They give some practical advice on the relationships between men and women.

Obviously, the author writes from and man's point of view. We, however, can very quickly see the value of his advice and its universal application.

Jealousy

The first verse in this section suggests that there is wisdom in not allowing jealousy to creep into a marital relationship. The intimacy of marriage requires trust. Jealousy begins to break down the trust within a marriage.

This verse contains some subtle psychology. Very often we suspect others of our own actions or thoughts. The husband who thinks he has reason to be jealous and suspects his wife of breaking the bond of trust is revealing his own untrustworthy actions or thoughts. It is through his jealousy that she will see her need to be jealous.

Giving Your Heart

As we read the Wisdom of Jesus Ben Sirach, we come to realize that his view of life is pessimistic and negative. Some of his advice must be spiritualized.

Certainly, in the marriage relationship we give our hearts to one another. In Hebrew culture the heart symbolized the center of life – not just the emotions. We give who we are – our essential beings – to the one whom we love.

This self-giving love is certainly Christ-like and essential in a Christian marriage, but this type of love must not be one that sacrifices the self in an addictive or compulsive manner. The foundation of a healthy marriage is not in giving of the self to the other <u>first</u>, but in the initial giving of the self completely to God. Only when we belong to God in love are we able to love as the one who first loved us.

Falling into the Trap

The first and third verses address prostitution. These two verses are not specifically for married men. They deal with sexual relationships.

The practice of prostitution reflected in the Old Testament contradicts the Biblical reasons for sexual relations – love, children, and mutual pleasure. Prostitution was performed for either money or as a religious act in many religions that surrounded the Israelites.

Common or "secular" prostitution developed early in Israel's history. There is some suggestion that prostitution was accepted without condemnation (Genesis 38.14-15, Joshua 2.4-16). Most of the evidence shows, however, that prostitution was disapproved in the Old Testament (Genesis 34.31, Leviticus 19.29, 21.7-9, Deuteronomy 22.21, and Amos 7.17). By the time of Jesus prostitution was condemned in Judaism (Matthew 21.32), and the use of prostitutes was not permitted by the early Church (1 Corinthians 6.15-16).

The common prostitute either waited for customers in public places or functioned as an innkeeper to whom men would come for food, lodging, and sexual satisfaction. She would exploit her beauty with her seductive dress. She would use persuasive language and maybe even sing.

Many of the religions surrounding the Israelites employed male and female prostitutes as a part of their practices. Though the Israelites never adopted this religious expression, some Israelites must have engaged in sexual relations with the prostitutes of other religions (Jeremiah 3.2).

Jesus Ben Sirach sees prostitution as both a moral and spiritual trap. Prostitution violates the Biblical reasons for sexual relations, entraps the person, and causes one to lose a healthy relationship with God.

Related to the warnings about prostitution is the warning against keeping company with singers. Songs had four basic purposes in the Old Testament cultures. Songs were used in preparation for battle (war chants), worship, magical incantations, and in "merrymaking." Songs for war were a part of the Israelite culture. Worship songs entered the religion of Israel later. Songs for magical incantations were condemned in the Israelite religion.

Songs used in "merrymaking" were often practiced licentiously and were connected with the seductive talk of prostitutes. Ben Sirach in verse four warns against this very practice.

Don't Look at Virgins

Verse five warns against staring at a virgin. By *virgin* Ben Sirach means a young girl at the age where she is capable of reproducing but who has not had sexual relations. *Virgin* can refer to young men, but this meaning is excluded by the context.

This warning reflects the value and protection given to virgins who could reproduce children for the family, provide workers for society, and carry on the name and line of a family. Stiff penalties were given to a man who violated a virgin (Exodus 22.16-17, Deuteronomy 22.28-9). Ben Sirach warns against the scandal, which accompanies the prolonged look, which leads to something more.

The Sights of the City

Verse seven does not directly apply to the marriage relationship. It is a warning against the seductive sights and sounds of the city and the potential temptations that Ben Sirach understood to exist in cities. This warning against the city streets and back alleys should be understood in the context of the prostitutes and singers who would be more readily available in such places.

Don't Look at Beautiful Women

Ben Sirach warns against lingering looks at a beautiful woman in verse eight. He is concerned that such looks will lead to foolish behavior and the man will fall in love with the beauty that belongs to another and be tempted into adultery.

Cuddling Another's Wife

Finally, Ben Sirach suggests that a man's familiarity with another man's wife will lead to destruction. Verse nine argues that such familiarity is never harmless and will lead to love.

Jesus Ben Sirach is concerned about the first step, which will eventually lead to embarrassment, scandal, destruction, or loss of God's blessing. This lesson is important for all of us: Stop and think. The first step leads down a path, which will result only in harm.

NOTES

John Wesley Slider

5 JESUS' TEACHING ON DIVORCE IN MATTHEW, MARK, AND LUKE

Mark 10.1-12

And He left there and went into the area of Judea and beyond the Jordan River; and again the crowd gathered around Him; and He taught them, as was His practice.

Pharisees approached Him, and to test Him they asked if it is permitted for a man to divorce his wife.

In answer He said to them, "What did Moses command you?"

They said, "Moses allowed for a written notice for a divorce."

Jesus said to them, "Because of your mean spirits this law was written for you; but from the very start of Creation He made them male and female. For this reason a man will leave his father and mother behind and be united to his wife, (8)and the two will be one body - not two bodies, but one body. So whatever God has united a man should not separate."

In the house the disciples again asked Him about this matter. He said to them, "Whoever divorces his wife and marries another commits adultery against his first wife; and if she divorces her husband and marries another, she commits adultery.

Matthew 19.1-12

When Jesus finished these words, He left Galilee and went into the area of Judea beyond the Jordan River; and large crowds followed Him, and He healed them there.

Pharisees approached Him to test Him and said, "Is it lawful for a man to divorce his wife for any reason?"

Answering He said, "Have you not read that from the very start of Creation He made them male and female?" He said, "Because of this a man will leave father and mother behind and be united to his wife, and the two will be in one body. Therefore they will no longer be two, but one body. So what God has united a man should not separate."

They said, "Then why did Moses command a man to give a written notice for a divorce?"

He said to them, "Moses permitted you to divorce your wives because of your mean spirits. From the start it was not like this. I say to you that whoever divorces his wife (except for sexual immorality) and marries another, commits adultery."

His disciples said to Him, "If this is how a relationship between a man and his wife is, then it is better not to marry."

But he said to them, "Not everyone can practice this word, but only the ones to whom it is given. For there are eunuchs who have been so from their mother's womb, and there are eunuchs who have been made eunuchs by men, and there are eunuchs who were made eunuchs by themselves for the Kingdom of Heaven. Those who are able to practice this should."

Luke 16.18

Everyone who divorces his wife and marries another wife commits adultery; and the woman who has been divorced from her husband commits adultery by remarrying.

Matthew 5.27-28, 31-32

You have heard it said, "You shall not commit adultery;" but I say to you that everyone who looks at a woman with desire for her has already committed adultery with her in his heart.

It is said, "Whoever divorces his wife must give her a written notice;" but I say to you that whoever divorces his wife (except on the basis of sexual immorality) makes her commit adultery; and whoever marries a woman who has been divorced commits adultery.

These four passages from the Synoptics contain Jesus' teaching on divorce. These four passages from three gospels form the basis for the Church's doctrine on this subject.

The Roman Catholic Church is the closest to Mark's version of this teaching. This tradition holds that there is no possibility of breaking the bonds of sacramental and consummated marriage. Ecclesiastical rulings do allow for the annulment of a marriage when either partner was not a full spiritual participant.

The Orthodox Church follows the Matthean version and allows for the possibility of breaking the marital bond because of the adultery of one partner. The innocent partner is allowed to remarry.

Anglican and Protestant churches vary greatly according to denomination and local practice. Most of these communions hold that Jesus' statements are not absolute but ideal.

The Context

There are three contexts in which Jesus' teachings on divorce should be interpreted. These are the Judaic religion in Jesus' day, the Greek and Roman culture of Jesus' day, and the early Church which preserved Jesus' teachings.

During Jesus' ministry there were two rabbinical "schools" – Shammai and Hillel. The more conservative Shammai School believed that the Mosaic Law allowed for divorce in the case of the wife's sexual misconduct. The more liberal Hillel School felt that a man could divorce his wife for any shameful or disgraceful act committed by her. An ultra conservative view is to be found in the community of Qumran, which taught that a man could divorce, but never remarry. These views were based on Deuteronomy 24.1-4 that was originally intended to protect the wife. In both Matthew and Mark the Pharisees that test Jesus are really asking to which rabbinical school He belongs.

The Gentiles of Greek and Roman culture during the time of Jesus did not have the restrictions on divorce that the Jews had. For one, Roman women had the ability to divorce their husbands and remarry. For another, there would not be as much economic pressure for a divorced woman to enter into a subsequent relationship. Jewish women in Jesus' day were forced to enter into another union – considered to be adulterous – in order to survive. Gentile women had less financial need to enter another union.

The early church found itself influenced by both Jewish and Greco-Roman culture. The Church had to interpret its message in the context of these two cultures. For example, some scholars suggest that the permission for divorce based on sexual immorality (*porneia*) in Matthew is a reflection of the early Church's struggle with the more relaxed endogamous and exogamous restrictions which the Gentiles had. According to this view the early Church at the Council of Jerusalem (Acts 15) sided with the Jewish endogamous and exogamous prohibitions as a minimum requirement for Gentiles to become Christians and banned "illegitimate marriage" or *porneia*.

Mark 10.1-12

Mark locates Jesus' teaching on divorce as Jesus has begun his journey toward Jerusalem and the cross. Mark has Jesus leaving Capernaum in the north, traveling south into Judea, and crossing to the eastern side of the Jordan River.

As usual a crowd gathers to hear Jesus and He begins to teach them. Some Pharisees in the crowd approach Jesus in order to test Him. Their interest is not to test His knowledge, but to determine to which rabbinical school He belongs – whether He is a liberal or conservative.

The Pharisees ask if divorce is permitted – specifically, if a man could divorce his wife. The question is nonsense in the context because among Jews divorce was already an accepted practice based on Deuteronomy 24.1-4.

Jesus brushes aside this ridiculous question with a question of His own in response: "What did Moses command you?"

They answer their own question and place Jesus in the position of either supporting or contradicting the Mosaic Law: "Moses allowed for a written notice of divorce."

Moses, indeed, allowed much more. A husband could divorce his wife with a written notice of divorce. The wife could remarry (and a man could marry a divorced woman), but the original husband could not remarry the wife he divorced. There is no limit placed on divorce or remarriage.

Jesus then enters into a discussion of the rule for divorce and the meaning of marriage. He moves the conversation from what is permitted to what is right.

Divorce is allowed because of the mean spirit or sinfulness of humanity, Jesus says in effect. Divorce is not a freedom granted by God's grace. It is a judgment on our sinfulness and an accommodation to what we do to one another in our sin.

Jesus turns to the Genesis account to explain God's intention for us. The reason for the male/female union in marriage is the reunion of the created order. It is God's creative action and initiative to make the two into one. The male/female union is not a consequence of sin but a part of God's will. To separate again the created order against God's will is wrong. Jesus places Himself in neither rabbinical school; and in fact, He is more conservative in upholding the principle of marriage in Genesis than even the Law of Moses in Deuteronomy 24.

The disciples are troubled by Jesus' teaching and later ask him to explain it further. Jesus contradicts the Law and social norms. The Law in Deuteronomy permitted divorce and remarriage. Jesus permits divorce but categorizes remarriage as adultery. Social norms during Jesus' day assigned responsibility for the divorce to the woman and allowed the man complete freedom. Jesus finds remarriage by the wife or the husband equally adulterous. Certainly, divorce with the intent to marry another is adultery – if not physically, then spiritually.

Jesus moves the conversation from our desire to find ways to free ourselves to act in any way without any responsibility to God or others. We need to follow God's call to act in accordance with the gift of creation. The call places a demand on us for we can no longer follow our will, but God's will.

The question is: What is God's will? Certainly, we would agree that to enter and exit marriages on a whim does not lead toward the abundant life that God offers us in Jesus Christ. Neither a legalistic "loophole" granting complete freedom to divorce and remarry, nor a legalistic requirement forbidding divorce, leads us to the life that God wills for us.

We all need to confess and repent of our sin and to throw ourselves on the mercy of God. Divorce, in the context of faith in God through Jesus Christ, can be a confession that the partners have not lived in accordance with God's will. Divorce can be a sign of repentance by which the partners acknowledge their failures before God and others. Divorce can set the partners free to experience the mercy of God anew.

Divorce is only a last resort after every attempt at reconciliation has been made and it is a step that should be made not for self but for the sake of others – the spouse and the children. Remarriage should not be banned under a rigid legalism, but divorce should not be contemplated with a remarriage in mind. For the person of faith, divorce and remarriage should be weighed in the context of the words and example of Jesus Christ who first loved us and gave Himself up for us.

Matthew 19.1-12

Matthew takes the story from Mark and makes some editorial changes that subtly change the message for his readers. These changes take the form of additional material and a reordering of the text.

The setting for the confrontation in Matthew is similar to that in Mark. Instead of teaching, Matthew says Jesus healed those who needed it.

The Pharisees ask Jesus if it is lawful for a man to divorce his wife for any reason. The additional *for any reason* suggests that they are seeking to discover to which rabbinical school Jesus belongs. This may reflect a particular interest of Matthew.

Jesus does not respond directly, but enters into a brief discussion of the Mosaic Law on divorce. Both the question and the response presuppose the permissibility of divorce. Jesus, however, focuses on God's will for marriage in Creation.

When Jesus says that man should not take apart what God has brought together, the Pharisees ask another question: "Why did Moses command a man to give a written notice of divorce?" In other words, if we are not to take apart what God has joined, why did Moses say we could?

Jesus responds that it is human sinfulness that created the need for divorce. Divorce is not God's will according to Genesis. Jesus avoids answering the initial question on the permissibility of divorce for any reason. He states that the only situation in which divorce and remarriage are permissible is in the case of sexual immorality. The sexual immorality or *porneia* could refer to the "illegitimate" marriages found in the early Church among Gentile converts. Whoever divorces and remarries except for the reason of sexual immorality or illegitimate marriage commits adultery.

The disciples suggest that this rule is too harsh and it is better not to marry. The idea that it is better not to marry also reflects a view of the early Church that expected the return of the risen Christ at any moment. Marriage would, in such a case, be an unnecessary or untimely union. Jesus suggests, however, that not everyone can remain unmarried. It is a gift to be able to remain unmarried until the coming of Christ.

Matthew then includes a teaching about eunuchs. Since this passage is unique to Matthew, it could be that it was Matthew's decision to connect it with the teaching on divorce.

Three classes of eunuchs existed at the time of the early Church – those born unable to have sexual relations, those rendered unable to have sexual relations (not an uncommon practice for government servants in the Middle East), and those Christians who chose not to have sexual relations or even chose self-castration (e.g. Origen) as an expression of their faith. Though the early Church did not discourage celibacy and welcomed eunuchs into its membership, self-castration was eventually seen as a barrier to ordination.

In this passage, Jesus upholds both marriage and celibacy. The consistent theme in His support of these two seemingly opposite situations is God's loving gift. Jesus commands neither marriage nor celibacy. Both are faithful responses to the love of God depending on how a person is called by God.

Jesus does treat marriage as a blessing. He avoids making a rule for Christians about divorce. The opportunity for remarriage is limited because remarriage tampers with God's reunion of Creation. In the case of a marriage destroyed by sexual immorality, remarriage is permitted for the innocent person.

It is not inconceivable that Matthew purposely placed Jesus' teaching on divorce in the context of His healings. Jesus' overall ministry could be seen as one of healing of relationships with God and with others. While marriage is a re-uniting of the oneness of the male and female "parts" of Creation, divorce may be understood as a breaking of this basic human relationship in which God is included according to Genesis. Jesus' ministry of healing then would presume that attempts are made to heal a broken marriage and to heal the persons within that marriage.

The healthy marriage between two spiritually healthy persons in which God is a part is the ideal. Because of our sinfulness, however, often times, there is only a choice between maintaining an unhealthy marriage that cannot be healed, and a divorce that allows the individuals to be healed.

Given the decision to divorce what should be the ultimate healing? We can imagine several components in the context of God's grace. We could anticipate the spiritual and emotional healing of the divorced husband and wife. We could hope for each to continue to grow in knowledge and love of God. We could pray that each would parent the children of the former marriage with a Christ-like spirit. We could be open to a new and healthy marriage that would nurture each former partner in faith. We could celebrate the time when both former partners could recognize and receive one another as a brother/sister in Christ, and begin have a healed relationship in that manner.

Luke 16.18

Luke has taken an isolated saying by Jesus on divorce, remarriage, and adultery and inserted it into his narrative. It is not connected to anything that precedes or follows.

This saying of Jesus on divorce and remarriage goes beyond the Law in its restrictions. A man is permitted to divorce, but not to remarry. A woman who has been divorced is not permitted to remarry. Jesus upholds monogamy and rejects successive polygamy.

The words of Jesus in Luke are similar to Paul's instruction in First Corinthians 7.10-13. Paul claims his teaching is not on his own authority, but is from the Lord. Paul's record is the earliest attestation of Jesus' teaching, but

Luke probably retains the more primitive form since Paul's writing reflects and Greek setting whereas Luke's context is Palestinian.

Paul charges wives not to separate from their husbands, or to either remain unmarried or reconcile if they are separated. A man should not divorce his wife; or a woman her husband.

Jesus in Luke's gospel does not necessarily forbid divorce, but does forbid successive marriages or successive polygamy. In doing so, Jesus was opposing a widespread practice in the Palestinian Judaism of His day. This opposition by Jesus is consistent with Luke's portrayal of Jesus' identification with and ministry to the downtrodden, outcast, and poor of society. Jesus' opposition to this practice of divorce in His society would give the woman greater security in a world where divorced women were forced into difficult relationships in order to survive after a divorce.

The saying in Luke comes from the Old Testament or Jewish point of view. Jesus' comment is based on the assumption that the husband is the one who takes action to divorce.

In the Old Testament adultery involved sexual intercourse of a married or engaged woman with someone other than her husband or betrothed. Death for both persons was the punishment for this violation of the seventh commandment.

The severity of the punishment suggests the seriousness of the act. Not only was adultery viewed as a crime against the offended husband, but also it was a crime that attacked the familial foundation of society.

Jesus goes beyond the Old Testament and equates divorce and remarriage with adultery. Jesus does not suggest that adultery can be justified in certain situations. Marriage is too important for that attitude.

Jesus never regards adultery as an unpardonable sin (John 7.53 - 8.11). Divorce and remarriage, therefore, never disqualifies a person from the love of God. It is a situation in which God's forgiveness and healing must be sought.

Matthew 5.27-28, 31-32

This teaching of Jesus appears in Matthew in a series of instructions on the Law during the Sermon on the Mount. In this expansion of the common source in Luke, Matthew shows Jesus not rejecting the Law but increasing its severity and thereby opening the Law to new interpretations.

In the society of Jesus' day it increasingly became a gimmick of some men to enter into temporary (short) marriages, thus giving a man license at the expense of women while at the same time protecting him from the charge of adultery. These men were maintaining the letter of the Law, but not the spirit.

Jesus first suggests that adultery is more than a matter of the Law; it is a matter of the spirit or the heart. A man who looks at a woman with desire has already committed adultery. Jesus makes the Law as strict as possible and by doing so uses it to defend women from exploitation. Adultery (for a man) is more than having sexual relations with a married woman. Adultery is looking with desire on any woman.

In the second section of this passage, Matthew shows Jesus condemning divorce. The man, who was the only one who could initiate divorce in the Jewish religion, becomes guilty of adultery in the divorce. The divorced woman had to turn for survival to another relationship that often did not include the status of marriage. The man, in this very real sense, makes his ex-wife commit adultery. In addition the one who marries a divorced woman commits adultery. The man is absolved from responsibility only if the wife has been unfaithful. The woman is not responsible in this case.

The Matthean Jesus is consistent with the teaching contained in chapter 19. In this passage, Jesus makes the Law stricter. He attacks the self-righteousness of a man who feels that all is right as long as he keeps all the rules. Jesus increases the severity of the rules in order for his listeners to look beyond them to examine the spirit behind the rules – the creation of healthy relationships in accordance with God's will.

NOTES

John Wesley Slider

6 1 CORINTHIANS 11.2-16 – MEN AND WOMEN IN THE COMMUNITY OF FAITH

I compliment you because you have kept me in mind in everything and you have held onto the traditions just as I handed them down to you. But I want you to know that the head of every man is Christ, and the head of a woman is the husband, and the head of Christ is God.

Any man who prays or speaks a word from God with his head covered disgraces his head; but any woman who prays or speaks a word from God with her head uncovered disgraces her head. It is as if she had shaved her head. For if a woman does not cover her head, then she might as well cut her hair; but if it is disgraceful for a woman to cut her hair or shave her head, then she should cover her head.

A man ought not to cover his head, for he possesses the image and glory of God; but a woman in the glory of a man; because the husband does not come from the woman, but the wife comes from the man. The husband was not created from the woman; but the wife was created from the man. Because of this a wife ought to have her husband's authority resting on her head – because of the angels. Nevertheless, in the Lord a wife is not independent of a man, neither is a husband independent of a woman; for just as a wife comes from a man, so also is a husband born of a woman; and all things come from God.

Decide these things among yourselves. Is it proper for a woman to pray to God with her head uncovered? Doesn't nature itself teach you that for a man wearing long hair is degrading to him, but for a woman wearing long hair is her glory? Her hair has been given to her instead of a covering. If anyone has a mind to be argumentative: Neither do we recognize any other practice, nor do God's churches.

Paul touches on the relationship between men and women in general and husbands and wives in particular in several of his writings. Many of his twentieth-first century readers have responded to Paul's views in a negative way – seeing him as outdated or simply wrong. This negative response is based on a superficial reading of Paul's letters and does not take into account his particular context.

In this chapter and the next we will look at two of Paul's teachings about the relationship between husbands and wives and see how they inform us about the Christian view of marriage. In this chapter we examine 1 Corinthians 11.2-16.

The question which arises while reading the passage is: Are Paul's teachings local and temporal or universal and eternal? The situation that Paul addresses – the attire of women who pray and prophesy in public worship – seems to be no longer relevant to us, but it certainly was relevant to the church at Corinth. Paul wrote to address a problem or issue in the church that was threatening the church. The situation is obviously local and temporal, but Paul's response establishes some universal and eternal Christian principles.

While the primary focus of Paul is worship, our focus is marriage. Paul's discussion, however, informs us about marital relationships.

The Situation Outside the Church

The city of Corinth, because of its location in Greece, had an excellent harbor and was, therefore, a wealthy center of trade and travel. Its wealth and the transient nature of much of its population helped give the city a reputation for sexual immorality and excess. In Paul's day, to call someone a Corinthian was to suggest that person was immoral and licentious.

Adding to the reputation of the city was the location of the temple to Aphrodite, the Greek goddess of love, in Corinth. The priestesses of the temple were actually sacred prostitutes. Prostitution, both sacred and secular, was very prevalent in Corinth.

There were some irregularities in the church at Corinth related to sexual morality and marital relationships. Prostitution was also an issue in the Corinthian church (1 Corinthians 6.9-20). Possibly some former prostitutes, either sacred or secular, were members of the church. Paul's comments about worship can be taken in this context. He is concerned in part that the women of the church might be confused with the prostitutes of the Temple of Aphrodite because of their attire in worship.

Women in Worship

Though our interest here is the relationship between husband and wife, Paul's concern was the role of women in worship. According to Jewish Law, women had no share in worship in the synagogue and the Temple. Greek women at Corinth, if they were not functioning as sacred prostitutes, were also kept in the background in the pagan temples since worship was an activity for the men.

Paul walks a fine line with the church at Corinth. He does not ban women's participation in or leadership of worship, and that is a break from his Jewish heritage. It is apparent that at Corinth some women were assuming leadership positions in the church. Paul shows that he has no problem with this development in other cities, but in Corinth it is an issue.

Paul sees the need to place some limits on the involvement of women in worship at Corinth because of the special conditions that existed outside the church at Corinth. For women to pray and speak at the Corinthian worship was fine with Paul. At issue at Corinth was: Can the women of the church take part in and lead worship without a covering? The issue is the attire of the women. No matter what limits Paul places on women in worship, he still affirms their equality.

Covering the Wife

Paul draws on his Middle Eastern background when he requires the women of the Corinthian church to wear a covering for her head when praying or speaking in public worship. Though Corinth was Greek, its people would have understood the significance of the covering because of the diversity of its cosmopolitan population.

In Paul's day the covering or veil was a sign of subordination. In the Middle East the *yashma* was worn over the head down to the feet with an opening for the eyes only. A respectable married woman never appeared in public without her *yashma*.

Not only was the covering a sign of subordination to the husband, it provided the married woman with security. Wearing the *yashma*, the woman would not be bothered and her modesty would be protected. It was bad manners to look at a veiled woman. It is possible that a young unmarried woman was allowed in public without a covering for her head, but when she was married she was required to have the full *yashma*. For a wife to be uncovered in public would bring shame to the husband. To take off the veil would be the same as taking off the wedding ring would be for us – if not more.

Paul, in his writings, assumes that the married state is normative and, therefore, he assumes the husband and wife relationship in his teachings. Essentially, Paul instructs the women to behave in worship like respectable married women. He instructs them to keep their covering intact so as not to act as a prostitute and bring shame on her husband. Remember that some Christian wives did not have Christian husbands, and the removal of the *yashma* would be a poor witness to these unconverted husbands.

Paul argues that for a woman to uncover her head and face would be the same as if she had shaved her head. Paul refers to the taking of a Nazirite vow in the Jewish religion that in part required the shaving of the head. A married woman could not assume such a vow of her own volition without dishonoring her husband. He argues that a wife indeed is her husband's reputation or honor (glory). In covering her head the woman was maintaining her husband's good reputation as well as her own.

Paul (consistent with positions on other issues that he took) would certainly argue that the Christian women of Corinth had the authority, power, and freedom to go uncovered in worship. His desire was that they exercise their Christian freedom responsibly. He wanted them to confirm to the acceptable cultural standards of decency. His appeal to nature is somewhat forced and is actually and appeal to common custom.

His attempt to argue that women should be veiled in worship "because of the angels" is also a stretch. Since his scriptural foundation is the creation story in Genesis, this reference to angels probably relates to Genesis 6.1-2.

Paul's interest is not in placing the wife under the husband's authority, but neither is his interest in changing the society around him. Paul stresses the essential partnership, interdependence, and mutuality of the husband and wife (see also 1 Corinthians 7.1-7) who are in Christ. He does this in the context of his opposition to divisiveness in the church and his interest in maintaining the good reputation and witness of individual Christians and the church in Corinth. This reputation is what set the church and Christians apart from the society around them; and was an important element in the proclamation of the good news of God in Jesus Christ.

NOTES

7 EPHESIANS 5.21-33 – THE MYSTERY IS GREAT

Be under the authority of one another out of respect for Christ.

Wives, be to your husbands as you are to the Lord, because the husband is the head of the wife as Christ is the head of the Church – He is Savior of the Body. As the Church is under the authority of Christ, so also should wives be to their husbands in all things.

Husbands, love your wives just as Christ loved the Church and gave Himself to her so that He might set her apart as sacred to God having made her clean with the washing of water in the word, so that He might dedicate the Church to Himself as honored, wearing nothing stained or wrinkled or damaged in any way, that she might be holy and faultless. So husbands ought to love their own wives as their own bodies. He who loves his wife loves himself, for no one ever disregards his own body, but feeds and takes care of it, just as Christ does for the Church, because we are part of His Body.

For a man leaves father and mother and is united to his wife, and the two are one body.

This mystery is great, and I am connecting it to Christ and the Church. Still, each of you love your wife as you love yourself, and let each wife respect her husband.

The Foundational Statement

The basic statement about relationships in the faith and in the Church is found in verse 21. Though translators have correctly connected this verse with the preceding section, it obviously is the basic statement that informs our interpretation of Paul's instruction on the relationship between husband and wife.

Love, not authority, is the essential character of all Christian relationships. Paul, however, encourages and mutuality of authority in all Christian relationships.

It is interesting that Paul does not encourage the individual to assume a position of authority over another. Rather, Paul urges the believer to place himself or herself under the authority of the other. The assumption of the servant role is done out of respect for Christ, Paul says. Paul describes Christ in Philippians 2 as the one who has authority, but who casts that authority aside and takes on the role of the servant for us. Our relationships with one another are not governed by our seeking authority over the other, but in giving ourselves in service to the other as Christ did.

Wives to Husbands

Paul encourages wives to relate to their husbands as Christ relates to the Church. This teaching is in the context of the mutuality of authority and service found in verse 21. As the Church is under the authority of Christ, who is both head and servant, so too the wife is under the authority of the husband. Wives are to respect their husbands, just as both husbands and wives respect Christ.

Husbands to Wives

Paul spends more time discussing the marital relationship in the direction of husband to wife. One could assume that given the cultural context, it was this side of the relationship that needed the most instruction from a Christian perspective.

Husbands are to love their wives as Christ loves the Church — sacrificially, in giving of the self, discarding authority, and becoming a servant. The husband honors his wife with this kind of love.

The love that is given to the wife by the husband is analogous, Paul says, to the husband's love for his own body. Indeed, the husband's love for his wife is love for his own body, since in marriage the husband and wife unite into one body.

The quotation from Genesis is also a reminder from Paul of the authority of the wife over the husband. In Genesis, it is the husband who goes to the woman and unites with her.

This relationship, Paul writes, is a mystery. The best parallel to the relationship between husband and wife is the relationship between Christ and the Church. He connects the two relationships because of the mutuality of service and self-giving that are found in both instances.

<u>NOTES</u>

John Wesley Slider

8 WEDDINGS AND MARRIAGE IN THE FREE METHODIST CHURCH

The Free Methodist Church of North America provides its pastors, members, and churches with doctrinal principles regarding marriage and rituals for the celebration of a marriage. The Biblical interpretations in the preceding chapters are consistent with the principles and ritual of the Free Methodist Church. ***The Book of Discipline***[2] and the ***Pastors and Church Leaders Manual***[3] contain statements regarding marriage and weddings in the context of the Christian Life and Journey. In paragraph 159 of The Book of Discipline the denomination states: "We commit ourselves to honor the sanctity of marriage and the family."

---

[2] ***2007 Book of Discipline***, Indianapolis, Indiana: The Free Methodist Publishing House, 2008.
[3] ***Pastor's and Church Leaders Manual***, Indianapolis, Indiana: Light and Life Communications, 2006.

The denomination gives a full statement of the principles regarding marriage and the nature of marriage in paragraph 3311.A of *The Book of Discipline*:

> *At creation God instituted marriage for the well being of humanity (Genesis 2:20-24; Mark 10:6-9). Marriage is the joining of one man and one woman into a lifelong relationship which the Scriptures call "one flesh." Sexual intercourse is God's gift to humanity, for the intimate union of a man and woman within marriage. In this relationship, it is to be celebrative (Hebrews 13:4).*
>
> *Marriage, between one man and one woman, is therefore the only proper setting for sexual intimacy. Scripture requires purity before and faithfulness within and following marriage. Likewise, it condemns all unnatural sexual behavior such as incestuous abuse, child molestation, homosexual activity and prostitution (1 Corinthians 6:9; Romans 12:6-27).*
>
> *We hold that marriage can only be the union of "one man and one woman" who have made a public covenant and vow before God and the state (Genesis 2:20-24; Mark 10:6-9). Therefore, it would be a breach of the doctrine of our church for ministers or members of the Free Methodist Church to conduct the marriage or blessing of a union between a same-sex or same-gender couple. In light of our beliefs, ministers and members of the Free Methodist Church shall not perform marriages or unions of same-sex or same-gender couples.*
>
> *We hold that our congregations are stewards of the church property. Performing a marriage or blessing between a same-sex or same-gender couple in any Free Methodist Church building or on any Free Methodist property would be a violation of consecrated Free Methodist property. Therefore, such blessings or marriages may not be performed at Free Methodist churches or on Free Methodist properties.*

> *Further, we believe that marriage the Free Methodist Church deems doctrinally acceptable, legal and appropriate should be safeguarded and supported by both the church and society and should be formalized with public vows. It is not enough for a couple to live together in private commitment; we believe that they are to covenant before God and the state.*

The Free Methodist Church commits its pastor, members, and churches to nurturing healthy marriages in paragraph 3311.B of the discipline:

> *The Free Methodist Church urges its people to enter the covenant of marriage prayerfully. In accordance with the apostle's command (2 Corinthians 6:14), we expect believers to marry only believers. Ministers are required to use diligent care when being requested to solemnize a marriage. It is contrary to the explicit teachings of the Scriptures to unite a believer with an unbeliever.*
>
> *Couples considering marriage should seek the wisdom of mature Christian leaders. Young couples contemplating marriage should seek parental consent.*
>
> *Ministers are required to use diligent care when being requested to solemnize a marriage. They shall not officiate at the marriage of any person under legal age. Pastors shall see that all candidates for marriage have received premarital guidance, using materials consistent with denominational teaching. We further encourage local churches to provide sex education and resources (seminars and retreats) preparing persons for marriage, to strengthen marriages and build Christian homes.*

The Free Methodist Church is committed to healing troubled marriages and helping person recover after divorce.

The denomination states its positions on healing, divorce, recovery, and remarriage in paragraphs 3311.C-F:

> *The church which is alive to God has spiritual resources for marriages in trouble. The chief resources are the renewing power of the Holy Spirit and the Word, prayer and the sacraments, counsel and support. Through the church's ministry, God can bring healing and reconciliation.*
>
> *Therefore, if our members find their marriage in crisis, we encourage them to seek the counsel of their pastor and submit to the guidance of the church. Professional counsel may be necessary. We recognize that domestic violence, emotional and/or physical, does occur in church-related families. It often jeopardizes the safety of a spouse or children and may threaten life itself. These family members need both spiritual and emotional healing (Malachi 2:13-16).*
>
> *When after counsel with the pastor, it is deemed that destruction of the home is imminent or has already taken place, Christians may separate. In such cases, the way to reconciliation must be kept open (1 Corinthians 7:10-11). Even when a marriage is violated by sexual infidelity, the partners are encouraged to work for restoration of the union.*
>
> *When one marriage partner is a Christian and the other a nonbeliever, we believe that the Christian may not for that reason divorce the unbelieving mate (1 Corinthians 7:12-13), because Christian love may redeem the unbeliever and unite the home in Christ (1 Corinthians 7:16).*
>
> *When a marriage is violated by sexual infidelity, the partners are encouraged to work for restoration of the union. Where reconciliation is impossible, a divorce may be allowed as inevitable (Matthew 5:32; 19:9).*
>
> *Desertion is the abandoning of a marriage without just cause. We believe that a person denies the faith when he/she deserts a spouse deliberately and for an extended period of*

time. When the desertion leads subsequently to divorce, the deserted partner is no longer bound by the marriage (1 Corinthians 7:15).

Where reconciliation is impossible in a troubled marriage, we acknowledge that divorce may be unavoidable (Matthew 5:32; 19:9). When marriages break down completely, we recognize that, in the words of Jesus, "hardness of heart" is implicit on one or both sides of the union (Matthew 19:3-8; Mark 10:5-9).

Though the Scriptures allow divorce on the grounds of adultery (Matthew 5:32) and desertion (1 Corinthians 7:10-16), they do not mandate divorce and we advise counsel with church leaders to seek other alternatives. One of these may be for both to live celibately.

Divorce always produces trauma. It is the breaking of a covenant, thus violating God's intention for faithfulness in marriage (Malachi 2:13-16). For this reason divorced persons should be helped to understand and remedy the causes for the divorce. They should seek pastoral counsel. Professional counsel may also be necessary. If unhealthy patterns of relating exist, the marriage partners must be helped to replace them with new attitudes and behaviors that are Christ-like (Colossians 3:1-15). Repentance and forgiveness are crucial to recovery. The goals of the process are personal healing and restoration to wholesome participation within the church. The church must extend its concern to family and others affected by the divorce.

A divorced member or one who is considering marriage to a divorced person must come under the authority, counsel and guidance of the church.

Persons who have been involved in divorce while in a state of unbelief shall not for that reason alone be barred from becoming members, even though they remarry. Similarly, believers are not prohibited from marrying a person who was divorced while an unbeliever. A member of the church divorced from an adulterous spouse or deserted by an unbelieving mate, after attempts at forgiveness and reconciliation have been rejected, may remarry (Matthew 5:31-32; 19:3-11; 1 Corinthians 7:15).

When a member divorces a spouse in violation of the Scriptures, or remarries without seeking the counsel or following the guidance of the pastor or the membership care committee, the committee shall review the case and recommend appropriate action to the local board of administration. Corrective action shall include removal from leadership, and may include suspension, or expulsion from membership. Exceptional cases may arise for which the pastor or the membership care committee can find no explicit direction in this Book of Discipline. In such cases, the pastor, after consultation with the membership care committee, shall confer with a superintendent.

NOTES

FREE METHODIST HANDBOOK: MARRIAGE AND WEDDINGS

9 PRACTICES AND GUIDELINES FOR WEDDINGS IN THE CHURCH

One of the functions of a church and a pastor is to lead the celebration of weddings. Every church should have some public statement on how weddings will be performed by its pastors and in its facilities. These statements should not be intended to restrict persons, but to raise the solemnity of the occasion and to insure the proper usage and maintenance of the church's facilities.

Most pastors and churches are pleased to contribute to the happiness of a bride and groom, their families, and their friends in a Christian wedding ceremony. Churches and pastors have, however, have different views on conducting weddings of non-believers and non-members.

The guidelines below are not intended to be unnecessarily restrictive or exclusionary. Rather, we hope that they will assist the couple in planning and enhance their memory of this event.

The Free Methodist Church places some requirements on pastors who are to conduct a wedding. These are found in paragraph 8200 of the discipline.

> *We will not charge for leading a marriage ceremony. Honoraria may be accepted. Publication of banns shall be made by proclaiming the intended marriage openly, in an audible voice, during divine service, in some church, chapel or place of public worship of the religious body to which the pastor who is to solemnize the marriage belongs, situated within the local municipality parish, circuit or pastoral charge where at least one of the parties to the intended marriage has resided for the period of eight days immediately preceding, at one or more services according to the requirements of the local jurisdiction.*
> *The pastor shall declare during the church service:*
> *I publish the banns of marriage between _____ of _____(place) and _____ of _____ (place). If any of you know cause or just impediment why these two persons should not be joined together in holy matrimony you are to declare it.*

Early Arrangements

The pastor should be contacted at the earliest possible time so that a tentative date may be selected and reserved for the wedding and rehearsal that does not conflict with the pastor's schedule. The couple should schedule the wedding at least three months prior to the projected wedding date. This will allow the pastor to place the event on his schedule of activities and for all other arrangements to be made.

As soon as the date is confirmed, the couple should set an appointment with the pastor. This one-hour session is for the purpose of pre-marital counseling. If the ritual or any administrative issues need to be discussed, a separate session should be scheduled. The couple and the pastor will determine if additional sessions are needed.

If any musicians are to participate in the ceremony it is suggested that they be contacted as soon as possible. The pastor is available to advise the couple in the selection of music.

It is the responsibility of the couple to insure that all legal requirements are completed. The pastor performing the ceremony must receive the marriage license on the day of the wedding. The pastor shall complete the license and post it no later than the first business day after the wedding.

The Officiating Minister

The Free Methodist Elder is ordained and licensed to conduct weddings. In a Free Methodist church if the wedding is to be conducted by another pastor in the church's sanctuary, the guest pastor shall contact the host pastor, and the host pastor shall extend the invitation to the pastor to be a guest.

Since the wedding ceremony in a Free Methodist church is a Christian worship service through which the presence and blessing of God – Father, Son, and Holy Spirit – are sought and experienced, no ministers, priests, officials scriptures, writings, or symbols of other religions or belief systems shall be a part of a ceremony conducted by the pastor or ministers of a Christian church. The Free Methodist pastor should not participate in any ceremonies involving ministers, priests, officials, scriptures, writings, or symbols of other religions or belief systems.

The exception to this policy would be ceremonies involving the Jewish faith. In this case, the pastor should discuss and develop a means by which the Christian witness is not compromised, but enhanced by the Jewish perspective. The couple planning such a ceremony should be allowed plenty of time for discussions between themselves and the pastor and rabbi.

Music and Musicians

The pastor's due counsel with the parties involved prior to marriage should include consultation with the organist or person in charge of music. Musicians should contact the officiating minister and discuss any relevant issues prior to rehearsal. Guest musicians should also familiarize themselves with the policies and guidelines regarding wedding music. The musicians should work with the couple in all decisions of music selection.

The service of marriage in the Church is provided for couples who wish to solemnize their marriage in a service of Christian worship. Concerning the selection of vocal or choral music to be performed in a service of Christian marriage, there is really only one simple rule. If the music is not appropriate for a Sunday morning worship service, the music is not appropriate for a service of Christian marriage. While there is a practice of using in weddings contemporary or popular love songs that express the romantic sentiment of the couple, such music is better suited for the rehearsal party or the reception.

Instrumental music of a wide variety is suited to the service of Christian marriage. Especially encouraged is music of a celebratory nature that can capture the mood of the occasion. The pastor in consultation with the organist/musicians is the final arbiter of the appropriateness of a musical selection for a service of Christian marriage.

Rehearsals

Normally the larger the wedding party or more formal the ceremony, the more likely a rehearsal will be needed. The couple will meet with the pastor prior to the rehearsal (or ceremony) to discuss the order of worship.

A rehearsal is normally held the evening before the day of the ceremony. It is expected that the rehearsal will begin at the appointed time and last for one hour. Though the officiating minister will try to be flexible, often times he or she has made other commitments and will need to complete the rehearsal in a timely manner.

Using Church Facilities

It must be remembered that a church's facilities are considered God's house by the congregation, and the behavior of the wedding party should reflect this belief at all times. The sanctuary is a special place to church members and should be treated with respect by all persons. Appropriate conduct and attire show this respect. Men should remove their hats while in the sanctuary out of respectful custom.

Smoking is not allowed in most church's buildings. Alcoholic beverages and other controlled substances usually are not allowed on Free Methodist church grounds or in the buildings. No such substances will be allowed during the rehearsal or ceremony. Out of custom food and drink are not allowed in the sanctuary.

Weapons of any sort are probably not allowed on a church's property unless they are properly secured in vehicles. Exceptions to this rule are the weapons of law enforcement officers and the ceremonial weapons for military weddings. The pastor of should be informed of any weapon and will make the final determination concerning the presence of a weapon.

Decorations should be appropriate. Most pastors request that the altar, pulpit, and lectern not be moved. Placement of the altar and its contents is under the direction of the pastor or his or her representatives. All decorations should be determined as early as possible and if there is any question the pastor should be asked as soon as possible.

Sometimes a fee is paid to the congregation for the use of its facility. This fee usually covers custodial services. Any damaged items should be shown to a manager of the facility or church before the wedding party leaves the building. Protective mats or plastic sheets must be placed under candles, potted plants, and watered greenery. The florist should be notified of this requirement. Rice poses a danger to birds and should not be allowed. Birdseed may be thrown outside the building, but the seeds need to be swept off of the walks and parking lot. Some wedding parties have begun the practice of releasing butterflies or blowing bubbles.

Minister's Assistant

A minister's assistant may be suggested for many weddings. This assistant is responsible to the pastor with administrative tasks and with various small and unseen tasks during the wedding. The minister's assistant should be available at the rehearsal and the ceremony to help the officiating minister.

Wedding Consultants

Sometimes couples hire a wedding consultant to assist them in planning and executing their wedding. Such consultants may or may not be arranged through the church.

While these professionals are often helpful, the couple should remember that the officiating minister leads the worship service. The officiating minister and the minister's assistant should be happy to have the assistance of the wedding consultant, but the officiating minister and minister's assistant will deal directly with the couple.

The pastor or other officiating minister is in charge of the wedding ceremony and rehearsal. If a wedding consultant is utilized, that consultant should make an appointment to coordinate his or her activities with the pastor and review all policies and guidelines.

Photographs and Videos

Most professional photographers and videographers are very capable and know what is expected of them during the ceremony. The couple is encouraged to hire professional photographers and videographers. These professionals know to consult with the officiating minister concerning their role during the service.

Family members are asked not to take photographs or to make videos of the service unless they are acting at the invitation of the couple and in consultation with the pastor. Many professional photographers and videographers have an exclusive agreement that they alone will take pictures and videos. Family members, though they mean well, do not know what is required of them and often cause a distraction during the worship.

The wedding ceremony is a worship service not a "photo-op." Photographers and videographers should be discrete in their work and not call attention to themselves. There should be no flashes or video lights used during the ceremony. Any part of the ceremony may be re-enacted after the service.

Photographers and videographers should be respectful of the schedule of the worship and of others. The timing of the service takes precedence over any photography. The officiating minister is available for a reasonable amount of time after the service for photographs.

Locations Other Than Sanctuaries

The pastor may conduct weddings at locations other than church sanctuaries. Homes, gardens, and wedding chapels may be used. The pastor shall not conduct a worship service in a location that is not conducive to the worship of God or consistent with the Christian witness.

Military Weddings

Each military service has its own traditions and regulations concerning weddings involving chaplains, ceremonies, uniforms, and military personnel. Couples are encouraged to examine the appropriate references and manuals.

Developing Trends

One of the many reasons that I transferred my orders from the United Methodist Church to the Free Methodist Church was that I noticed the developing trends in the United Methodist Church with regards to social issues — including the denomination's stand on same-sex marriage. I see a future where the United Methodist Church will endorse and approve such marriages.
 The Free Methodist Church has a better grasp of the Biblical concept of marriage. I believe that the Free Methodist Church will remain true to the Biblical

understanding of marriage. It is in this denomination where I found a home when I transferred in 2010.

In 2014 as I look at the American culture, I am saddened by the developing trends with regard to same-sex marriage. I anticipate in the near future a social context in which states and perhaps the federal government will either refuse to define marriage at all, or define marriage to include same-sex couples. A lack of a definition of any kind will open society to marriages of all sorts.

If this "neutral" position were not bad enough, there are increasing pressures through the judicial system to put pressure on Christians to provide services for weddings to which they object on religious grounds. Included in this are "wedding chapels" that are not churches, but services of Christian ministers. For this reason the church that I serve (following my advice) stopped operating a "wedding chapel" or public service. I shall no longer perform weddings outside the membership of the congregation.

The problems do not stop there, however. As a part of officiating a wedding in the Commonwealth of Kentucky, I act as an agent of the state by signing the certificate of marriage. If I act as an agent of the state, am I required to operate under the rules and definitions of the state? Will I be forced to perform weddings that are against my beliefs and the ***Discipline*** of my denomination?

I also serve as the chaplain for the St. Matthews Police Department. Will I (and all chaplains) be forced to perform weddings that are against my beliefs and the ***Discipline*** of my denomination?

All Christian pastors will need to wrestle with these questions as society moves toward a less than favorable environment for Biblical Christian beliefs.

NOTES

10 MARRIAGE COUNSELING AND IMPORTANT ISSUES TO ADDRESS

A pastor performs a marriage ceremony after due counsel with the parties involved. The decision to perform the ceremony shall be the right and responsibility of the pastor in accordance with the laws of the state and practices of the church.

Marriage counseling will focus on the theological, spiritual, emotional, physical, financial, and social issues of marriage. The session or sessions shall deal with any past issues or present expectations that could hamper the marriage. Marriage counseling is intended to be a positive time for the couple to examine important issues. Counseling should be approached with openness and in a prayerful manner.

Theological and Spiritual Issues

Before marriage couples should discuss religious issues. This booklet has outlined the important Biblical foundations and understandings of marriage. Reading a book, having an ordained minister preside, and holding the wedding ceremony in a sanctuary or religious setting, will not insure that a marriage will last.

Religious considerations are important. One could say in this regard, "What you see is what you get." Do not expect marriage to convert one partner to the religious views of the other partner.

Religion, or lack of religious affiliation, speaks to a person's ultimate system of values. Religious differences can very well be the cause of conflict in a marriage and a family. The more one's faith means to a person, the more that person needs a spouse with similar system of belief.

Conflict may occur when the husband and wife are of different religions, different denominations, different perspectives, or even different levels of adherence to religious values. Religious differences (for example if one partner is Christian, and the other Jewish), could lead to conflict over which religious holidays are celebrated and how the celebration takes place; where the couple will worship, if they wish to worship together; and in what faith the children will be raised. Pressures on the marriage for one partner to convert could come from either side of the family. These conflicts and pressures could eventually lead to resentment and anger. If a compromise is reached, it is never equal.

There can also be important differences when the husband and wife are Christian, but are from different denominations. Worship styles and belief systems vary between denominations. Though to a lesser extent, the same conflicts and pressure exist in this situation as in the case where the husband and wife are of different religions. Such is the case as well with different religious perspectives (e.g. charismatic, fundamentalist, conservative, liberal, etc), and adherence (committed or nominal).

Emotional Issues

Again, the rule-of-thumb is "What you see is what you get." Do not expect marriage to mature a person or help a person grow out of emotional problems.

Each person contemplating marriage should carefully look at their own family life and that of their prospective spouse. The role models a person has for the relationship between husband and wife will either indicate the patterns a person will follow in his or her own marriage or will indicate the fears and concerns a person brings into a marriage.

Serious emotional problems should be addressed prior to marriage. A spouse should know if his or her prospective partner has a history of emotional problems or has issues with which he or she needs to address. Marriage often will worsen a person's emotional and psychological challenges.

Physical Issues

Physical and medical differences from types of diet to hereditary conditions are important points of discussion. A prospective spouse should be aware of the challenges of any handicapping conditions and be aware of how to deal with them. Hereditary conditions could have an impact on whether or not a couple decides to have children. Other concerns such as dietary, smoking, and drinking habits may be overlooked during dating, but may cause conflict or concern within a marriage.

Financial Issues

Finances are the greatest source of continuing conflict in a marriage. Bringing excessive debt into a marriage should be avoided. The rule-of-thumb is "What is mine, is ours." This applies to liabilities as well as assets.

It is strongly recommended that all couples should develop a disciplined and equal partnership in dealing with the finances of the family. Furthermore, a couple marrying in their twenties should not try to obtain everything all at once.

Here is a basic and general guideline for financial planning by a young couple:

1. Determine who will be the bookkeeper for the family.
2. Wait three days before making any large purchase.
3. Do not open any new credit card accounts and close all current credit card accounts.
4. Establish an emergency savings account with the first goal being the accumulation of $1,000 and the second goal being three two six months of expenses.
5. Pay off all debts using the "snowball" effect - setting a monthly amount paying minimums on all but the smallest, then when the smallest debt is paid, using that amount to accelerate payment on the next smallest.
6. Establish a savings account for purchasing a house. Do not purchase a house unless there is 20% of the purchase price in the account. When purchasing a house, get a 15 year fixed mortgage.
7. Do not buy any new cars. A car is not an investment. A car begins to depreciate when you sign the purchase agreement. Vehicles loose 60% of their value in the first four years.
8. Establish a budget under the following guidelines: For a couple with a net spendable income after

taxes and tithe of $32,445 ($45,000 gross) 30% for housing, 13% for food, 12% for automobiles, 5% for insurance, 5% for debt reduction, 5% for entertainment, 5% for clothing, 5% for savings, 4% for medical and dental, 5% for investments, and 5% for miscellaneous expenses.

Children are expensive. If a couple waits until they can afford to have children to have children, they will never have children. Besides one another, the greatest blessing a couple can receive is to have children. Raising children requires creative ways to budget resources, but by God's grace a family will thrive.

Children

A couple should enter into marriage with some general understanding about the timing and number of children, though there are always pleasant surprises along the way. There may be children from a previous marriage that will be incorporated into the family immediately. Custody and relationships with prior spouses need to be understood and approached in a mature and non-competitive manner. Couples who cannot have children may want to adopt.

Social Issues

Several social factors will need to be considered prior to marriage. Racial, ethnic, and language differences will need to be considered. Religion has already been discussed, but couples should also discuss educational levels and expectations for themselves and any children. Career choices are also important. Entertainment and recreational choices also need to be examined.

The couple should seek social activities that bring them closer and support their marriage. A special basketball game with the guys or an occasional night out with the girls may be a welcome change of pace, but activities in which the spouse cannot or will not share will create a sense of separation. One must remember, the two are made one.

Legal Issues

Each person should be open and disclose and past or present legal situations. Though a "police check" is not suggested, it is important to be open and honest. Any legal entanglements that could damage the marriage should be shared.

Expectations

No one wants to live in the past, but often times we do repeat the past in our relationship. The past is our starting point. Our expectations are the goal. In between is the journey. In order to commit to another person for the journey of marriage, one must have a good understanding of who that person is.

The best advice is: "No surprises!" Information shared prior to a marriage is much more easily understood, forgiven, and assimilated than the same information one-year or ten years later. Secrecy suggests a lack of emotional commitment to a relationship. Trust is critical to a marriage. A husband and wife should have a complete trust in one another. Trust begins with an open and honest sharing of past issues and present expectations.

Expectations for Commitment and Fidelity

Recent studies have suggested that men and women bring into their marriages different expectations concerning fidelity based on roles each played in primitive society. Men tend to place a high value sexual fidelity in their wives. Men also tend to seek out younger women and sometimes numerous relationships. Women seem to place a high value on emotional fidelity in their husbands and will often seek unions with stable, powerful, established, older men.

Leaving aside the moral issues involved, one can see how these conflicting expectations arose in primitive society. The primitive male sought assurances that the children of his mate were actually his offspring. In addition, in a primitive society a family's children provided workers, hunters, and warriors. The dominant male of the family would seek to produce as many offspring as possible to increase the chances for survival of the family. The seemingly hypocritical goals of the primitive male, therefore, were sexual fidelity to him from as many unions with productive females as he could support.

The primitive female, however, sought assurances that she and her offspring would be secure. She would seek out the strongest and most powerful male who would be emotionally committed to her and her children. Even as the lines between roles of males and females become more blurred in modern society, we can still see these primitive values and expectations exerting themselves. Men and women are different!

Christianity has a higher standard of conduct and commitment than simply what as evolved from primitive societies. A Christian marriage is a partnership between a man and a women who are lovingly, equally, and fully committed to each other, having given themselves completely to the other in a Christ-like manner.

Expectations for Communicating Love

In *The Five Languages of Love,* Dr. Gary Chapman suggests that because of past experiences and examples within their own families, individuals express love and understand how love is expressed to them in different "languages." He outlines five primary languages of love - Words of Affirmation, Quality Time, Receiving Gifts, Acts of Service, and Physical Touch. It is important to understand the different ways in which love is expressed and understood by each partner in a marriage. Learning to express your love to your husband or wife is critical.

One spouse or the other may understand love in terms of Words of Affirmation such as compliments, expressions of gratitude and appreciation, praise, or affirmation. Positive words, both written and spoken, are highly valued by these persons and make them feel loved.

A partner in a marriage may understand he or she is loved through quality time or the giving of one's undivided and focused attention. They may feel loved most in quiet times of togetherness or quality conversation. Eye contact, not conversing while doing something else, refusing to interrupt - these communicate the spending of quality time.

Maybe a husband or wife will feel loved by receiving gifts. Gifts are symbols of love and have emotional value beyond any material value. A gift need not be expensive, but should be a gift of the self to the other. Physical presence may be a gift in itself.

Acts of Service may be the way by which a husband or wife feel loved. Acts of Service are those things that your spouse would like you to do. These acts could be simple things such as letting out the dog, mowing the grass, or balancing the checkbook.

Finally, Physical Touch may be a means by which a partner understands he or she is loved. Physical touching in a marriage ranges from sexual intercourse to holding hands. Hugs during a crisis, or an embrace in a moment of joy, speak love.

Of course, we can see that each language should be spoken and heard in a marriage, but each of us has a primary language. It is important to learn the language of our husband or wife and to become fluent. We must learn to say, "I love you."

Questions to Ask and Answer

Theological, Spiritual, and Religious

1. Where will we worship and how often?
2. What religious holidays will we observe and how will we observe them?
3. How will the children be raised?
4. How do we view God's role in our lives and marriage?
5. How do we view the role of the husband and wife in making religious decisions?
6. What external pressures will religious expectations cause on our marriage?

Emotional and Psychological

1. What was the past family life of each person?
2. What were the roles of the father and mother in the family?

3. Are there any emotional or psychological issues in the past or present?

Physical and Medical

1. Are there any physical conditions that may have an impact on the relationship?
2. Are there any handicapping conditions for which a spouse will need special training?
3. Are there any dietary differences?
4. Does either partner smoke or drink excessively or have any addiction?

Financial

1. Who is the bookkeeper?
2. Are there any debts coming into the marriage?
3. What are the financial goals of our marriage?
4. Will we be one income or two now and when we have children?

Children

1. How many children would we like to have and when should we try to have them?
2. Are there any children from previous relationships and what impact will that have on every aspect of our marriage?
3. Would we consider adopting children?
4. What is the role of the husband and wife in raising children?

Social

1. Do we face any challenges related to race, ethnic background, or language?
2. What are our educational levels and could this be a source of friction?
3. Do we understand each other's career pattern?
4. What do we enjoy doing together?
5. Are there any activities that would exclude or cause separation?

Legal

1. Are there any present or past legal situations in which either persons finds himself or herself?
2. Are there any previous marriages, alimony payments, or child support payments?
3. Is there any situation that needs to be explained now before the marriage takes place?

What Your Grandmother Would Tell You

Premarital counseling in its essence is simple. It is advice that your grandmother would give.

1. What you see is what you get.
2. What is mine is ours.
3. Children don't fix marriages.
4. Do not surprise me.
5. Men and women are different.
6. Learn to say, "I love you."

NOTES

11 THE SOLEMNIZATION OF MATRIMONY – THE FREE METHODIST CHURCH

The *2007 Book of Discipline of the Free Methodist Church* not only contains the doctrine and rules of the denomination, but also its rituals. Paragraph 8210 of the *Discipline* offers the following ritual for marriage:

At the time set, the man and woman to be married shall stand together facing the pastor, the woman on the man's left, and the pastor shall say:

Dearly beloved, we are gathered together here in the sight of God and the presence of these witnesses to join together _____ and _____ in holy matrimony. Marriage is an honorable estate, instituted by God in the time of creation for the wellbeing of mankind. It is safeguarded by the laws of Moses, affirmed by the words of the prophets, and hallowed by the teachings of our Lord Jesus Christ. Marriage is a union close and enduring, a relationship in which a man and a woman forsake all others to become one flesh. This abiding union illustrates the holy relationship between Christ and His church. Marriage is therefore not to be entered into by any lightly, but reverently, soberly and in the fear of God.

Addressing the man and woman, the pastor shall say:

_____ and _____, I charge you both as you stand in the presence of God to remember that covenant love alone will avail as the foundation of a happy and enduring home. Let Christ, who was loyal to His own unto death, be your example. Let the Apostle Paul be your teacher, who wrote: "Love is patient and kind; love is not jealous or boastful; it is not arrogant or rude. Love does not insist on its own way; it is not irritable or resentful; it does not rejoice at wrong, but rejoices in the right. Love bears all things, believes all things, hopes all things, endures all things." If you keep this steadfast love ever before you and, remaining faithful to each other, resolutely endeavor to fulfill the vows you now will make, God's blessing will be upon you, and the home you establish will endure through life's every change.

The pastor shall say to the man, using his Christian name:

_____, will you have _____ to be your wedded wife, to live together in the holy estate of matrimony? Will you love her, comfort her, honor and keep her, in sickness and in health; and forsaking all others, keep yourself only for her, so long as you both shall live?

The man shall answer: I will.

The pastor shall say to the woman, using her Christian name:

_____, will you have _____ to be your wedded husband, to live together in the holy estate of matrimony? Will you love him, comfort him, honor and keep him, in sickness and in health, and forsaking all others, keep yourself only for him, so long as you both shall live?

The woman shall answer: I will.

The pastor shall say:

Who gives _____ to be married to _____?

The father or other family member of the woman, or whoever gives her in marriage, shall answer: I (We) do.

The pastor, receiving the hand of the woman from her father or other sponsor, shall cause the man with his right hand to take the woman by her right hand, and say after the pastor:

I, _____, take you, _____, to be my wedded wife, to have and to hold, from this day forward, in plenty and in want, in joy and in sorrow, in sickness and in health, to love and to cherish till death us do part, and thereto I pledge you my faith.

They shall loose their hands, and the woman, with her right hand, shall take the man by his right hand, and shall likewise say after the pastor:

I, _____, take you,_____, to be my wedded husband, to have and to hold, from this day forward, in plenty and in want, in joy and in sorrow, in sickness and in health, to love and to cherish till death us do part, and thereto I pledge you my faith.

They again shall loose hands. The groomsman may give to the pastor a ring, which the pastor in turn will give to the groom, who will put it upon the third finger of the bride's left hand and, holding the ring, shall say after the pastor:

This ring I give you in token and pledge of our constant faith and steadfast love.

In case of a double ring ceremony, the pastor shall receive the other ring from the bridesmaid and shall deliver it to the woman to put upon the third finger of the man's left hand. The woman, holding the ring there, shall say after the pastor:

This ring I give you in token and pledge of our constant faith and steadfast love.

The pastor shall say:

Let us pray. O Eternal God, creator and preserver of all mankind, giver of all spiritual grace, the author of everlasting life: send Your blessing upon this man and this woman whom we bless in Your name; that they, living faithfully together, may surely perform and keep the vow and covenant between them made, and may ever remain in perfect love and peace together, and live according to Your laws through Jesus Christ our Lord. Amen.

The pastor shall say:

Forasmuch as _____ and _____ have consented together in holy wedlock and have witnessed the same before God and this company and have pledged their faith each to the other and have declared the same by joining hands (and by giving and receiving a ring), therefore, by the authority granted to me as a minister of Jesus Christ, I pronounce that they are husband and wife together, in the name of the Father, and of the Son, and of the Holy Spirit. Those whom God has joined together, let not man put asunder. Amen.

The man and woman then kneel or bow, and the pastor shall pray over them an extemporaneous prayer, prepared especially for the two of them. The man and woman shall stand, and the pastor shall pronounce over them the following benediction:

Go forth into the world in peace. Be of good courage. Hold fast to that which is good. Render to no one evil for evil. Strengthen the faint hearted. Support the weak. Help the afflicted. Show honor to all. Love and serve the Lord, rejoicing in the power of the Holy Spirit. And the blessing of God Almighty, the Father, the Son, and the Holy Spirit, be upon you and remain with you forever. Amen.

NOTES

John Wesley Slider

12 A SERVICE OF MARRIAGE FROM THE METHODIST CHURCH

The Free Methodist ritual provides an appropriate ceremony for the solemnization of a marriage. If the couple wants a more formal ritual there is one available from the 1964 ***Book of Worship of the Methodist Church***. The Methodist Church is a predecessor to the United Methodist Church that was formed by merger in 1969. This ritual is consistent with Free Methodist practices.

This service may begin with a prelude and/or processional and conclude with a postlude and/or recessional.
When the sacrament of the Lord's Supper is requested, this service should be provided at a time other than the service of marriage.
At the appointed time the minister shall say:

Dearly beloved, we are gathered together here in the sight of God, and in the presence of these witnesses, to join together this man and this woman in holy matrimony; which is an honorable estate, instituted of God, and signifying unto us the mystical union which exists between Christ and His Church; which holy estate Christ adorned and beautified in

Cana of Galilee. It is therefore not to be entered into unadvisedly, but reverently, discretely, and in the fear of God. Into this holy estate these two persons come now to be joined. If any man can show just cause why they may not lawfully be joined together, let him now speak, or else hereafter forever hold his peace.

I require and charge you both, as you stand in the presence of God, before whom the secrets of all hearts are disclosed, that, having duly considered the holy covenant you are about to make, you do now declare before this company your pledge of faith, each to the other. Be well assured that if these solemn vows are kept inviolate, as God's Word demands, and if steadfastly you endeavor to do the will of your heavenly Father, God will bless you marriage, will grant you fulfillment in it, and will establish your home in peace.

_____, wilt thou have this woman to be thy wedded wife, to live together in the holy estate of matrimony? Wilt thou love her, comfort her, honor and keep her, in sickness and in health; and forsaking all other keep thee only unto her so long as ye both shall live?

The man shall answer: I will.

The minister shall say:

_____, wilt thou have this man to be thy wedded husband, to live together in the holy estate of matrimony? Wilt thou love him, comfort him, honor and keep him, in sickness and in health; and forsaking all other keep thee only unto him so long as ye both shall live?

The woman shall say: I will.

The minister shall say:

Who giveth this woman to be married to this man?

The father of the woman or whoever gives her in marriage shall answer as appropriate: I do (Her mother and I do, Her family does, etc.).

The father of the woman shall be seated. Scripture may be read at this point. If the couple desires scripture lessons to be read, they may chose from the following: Genesis 1.26-28, 31a; Isaiah 42.1-7; Isaiah 55.10-13; Isaiah 61.10-62.23; Isaiah 63.7-9; Matthew 22.35-40; Mark 2.18-22; Romans 12.1-2, 9-18; 1 Corinthians 13; Colossians 3.12-17; 1 John 3.18-24; 1 John 4.7-16.

Then the minister shall receive the hand of the woman and give her hand to the man and have the man repeat after him:

I, _____, take thee, _____, to be my wedded wife, to have and to hold, from this day forward, for better, for worse, for richer, for poorer, in sickness and in health, to love and to cherish, till death us do part, according to God's holy ordinance; and thereto I pledge thee my faith.

Then the minister shall have the woman repeat after him:

I, _____, take thee, _____, to be my wedded wife, to have and to hold, from this day forward, for better, for worse, for richer, for poorer, in sickness and in health, to love and to cherish, till death us do part, according to God's holy ordinance; and thereto I pledge thee my faith.

The man and the woman shall approach the altar. Then they may give to each other rings, or the man may give to the woman a ring. The minister shall receive the ring or rings and shall say,

The wedding ring is the outward and visible sign of an inward and spiritual grace, signifying to all the uniting of this man and this woman in holy matrimony, through the Church of Jesus Christ our Lord. Let us pray.

Bless, O Lord, the giving of these rings (this ring), that they who wear them (she who wears it) may abide in Thy peace, and continue in Thy favor; through Jesus Christ our Lord. Amen.

The minister shall deliver the proper ring to the man to put on the third finger of the woman's left hand. The man shall repeat after the minister:

In token and pledge of our constant faith and abiding love, with this ring I thee wed, in the Name of the Father, and of the Son, and of the Holy Spirit. Amen.

The minister shall deliver the proper ring to the woman to put on the third finger of the man's left hand. The woman shall repeat after the minister:

In token and pledge of our constant faith and abiding love, with this ring I thee wed, in the Name of the Father, and of the Son, and of the Holy Spirit. Amen.

If a unity candle is being used it may be lit by the man and woman at this time. A solo or other musical interlude is appropriate. Then the minister shall place his right hand on the joined hands of the man and woman and say:

Forasmuch as _____ and _____ have consented together in holy wedlock, and have witnessed the same before God and this company, and thereto have pledged their faith each to the other and have declared the same by joining hands and by giving and receiving rings (a ring); I pronounce that they are husband and wife together, in the Name of the Father, and of the Son, and of the Holy Spirit. Those whom God hath joined together, let not Man put asunder. Amen. Let us pray.

O Eternal God, Creator and Preserver of all Mankind, Giver of all spiritual grace, the Author of everlasting life: Send they blessing upon this man and this woman, whom we bless in Thy Name; that they may surely perform and keep the vow and covenant between them made, and may ever remain in perfect love and peace together, and live according to Thy laws. Look graciously upon them, that they may love, honor, and cherish each other, and so live together in faithfulness and patience, in wisdom and true godliness, that their home may be a haven of blessing and a place of peace; through Jesus Christ our Lord. Amen.

The congregation may join in saying the Lord's Prayer or it may be sung at this time.

The minister shall say:

God, the Father, the Son, and the Holy Spirit, bless, preserve, and keep you; the Lord graciously with His favor look upon you, and so fill you with all spiritual benediction and love that you may so live together in this life that in the world to come you may have life everlasting. Amen.

The minister shall invite the man and woman to kiss and then introduce the couple.

NOTES

FREE METHODIST HANDBOOK: MARRIAGE AND WEDDINGS

13 A RITUAL FOR THE REAFFIRMATION OF THE MARRIAGE COVENANT

The occasion may arise for a couple or group of couples to reaffirm or renew the vows of their marriage covenant. This opportunity may come on a significant anniversary. It may be the result of reconciliation of a husband and wife after lengthy counseling. Possibly, a group of couples may choose to renew their vows as a part of a time of marriage enrichment. The pastor and the church family should be involved in renewing and reaffirming healthy relationships through a ritual of reaffirmation. Through this ritual, the couple not only recommit themselves to one another; they also recommit themselves and their marriage to God, and re-invite God into their marriage. **The United Methodist Book of Worship** (1992) provides an order for the reaffirmation of the marriage covenant that is appropriate for Free Methodist pastors and churches.

This order may be a response to the Word during regular congregational worship or as a separate service. If children or grandchildren of the couple(s) are present, they may participate by blessing the marriage, reading scripture lessons, singing or playing music, or making a witness in their own words.

When the couple(s) is/are gathered the pastor begins by saying:

Friends, we are gathered together in the sight of God to witness and bless the reaffirmation of the marriage covenant, which was established by God, who created us male and female for each other. With his presence and power Jesus graced a wedding at Cana of Galilee, and in his sacrificial love gave us the example for the love of husband and wife.

The couple(s) face each other, join hands, and speak directly to each other, repeating the vows, phrase by phrase, after the pastor – first husband to wife, then wife to husband:

In the name of God, and with a thankful heart, I once again declare that I, _____, take you _____, to be my wife/husband to have and to hold from this day forward, for better, for worse, for richer, for poorer, in sickness and in health, to love and to cherish, until we are parted by death. This is my solemn vow.

The pastor shall then invite the gathered people to pray:

Let us pray. Eternal God, Creator and preserver of all life, author of salvation, giver of all grace: Bless and sanctify with your Holly Spirit _____ and _____ who have reaffirmed their marriage covenant. Enable them to grow in love and peace with you and with each other all their days, that they may reach out in concern and service to the world; through Jesus Christ our Lord. Amen.

The pastor shall then bless the marriage:

O God, you have so consecrated the covenant of Christian marriage that in it is represented the covenant between Christ and his Church. Send therefore your blessing upon _____ and _____, that they may surely keep their marriage covenant, and so grow in love and godliness together that their home may be a haven of blessing and a place of peace; through Jesus Christ our Lord. Amen.

The pastor shall conclude the ceremony by saying to the couple(s):

God the Eternal keep you in love with each other, so that the peace of Christ may abide in your home. Go to serve God, your family, and your neighbors in all that you do.

NOTES

14 A SERVICE FOR THE BLESSING OF A CIVIL MARRIAGE

There could be many circumstances that would cause a couple to become married outside the Church and then seek the blessing of their civil marriage. It could very well be that a couple was married before becoming followers of Christ, and later after becoming Christians, want to have their civil wedding blessed as an expression of their new faith.

Whatever the circumstances the pastor and congregation should not be judgmental, but loving and caring when a couple seeks to have their civil ceremony blessed. The pastor should provide appropriate counseling prior to the service.

The couple may choose to use the complete wedding service or a special service for blessing their civil marriage. **The United Methodist Book of Worship** (1992) provides an order for the blessing of a civil marriage that is appropriate for Free Methodist pastors and churches.

This order may be a response to the Word during regular congregational worship or as a separate service. If children of the couple are present, they may participate by blessing the marriage, reading scripture lessons, singing or playing music, or making a witness in their own words.

When the couple is gathered the pastor begins by saying:

Friends, we are gathered together in the sight of God to witness and bless the marriage of _____ and _____, who have been married by the law of the state/commonwealth. Now in faith they come before the witness of the Church to declare their marriage covenant and to acknowledge God's good news for their lives.

The pastor shall then invite the gathered people to pray:

Let us pray. Eternal God, Creator and preserver of all life, author of salvation, giver of all grace: Bless and sanctify with your Holly Spirit _____ and _____ who come now seeking your blessing of their marriage covenant. Grant that they may reaffirm their vows to each other in the strength of your steadfast love. Enable them to grow in love and peace with you and with each other all their days, that they may reach out in concern and service to the world; through Jesus Christ our Lord. Amen.

The pastor then shall address the couple:

_____ and _____ you have come here today to seek the blessing of God and of the Church upon your marriage.

The pastor shall ask the wife:

_____, you have taken _____ to be your lawful husband. Now you wish to declare, before God and this congregation, your desire that your married life should be according to God's will. I ask you, therefore, will you love him, comfort him, honor and keep him, in sickness and in health, and forsaking all others, be faithful to him as long as you both shall live?

The wife shall answer: I will.

The pastor shall ask the husband:

_____, you have taken _____ to be your lawful wife. Now you wish to declare, before God and this congregation, your desire that your married life should be according to God's will. I ask you, therefore, will you love her, comfort her, honor and keep her, in sickness and in health, and forsaking all others, be faithful to her as long as you both shall live?

The husband shall answer: I will.

The pastor shall ask the husband and wife to join left hands and say:

These rings are the outward and visible sign of an inward a spiritual grace, signifying to all the union between Christ and his Church.

The pastor shall then place his hand on the couple's joined hands and say:

Bless, O Lord, the wearing of these rings that they who wear them may live in your peace and continue in your favor all the days of their lives; through Jesus Christ our Lord. Amen.

The pastor shall continue to keep his hand of the couple's hands, or he may wrap a stole around their joined hands, and say:

_____ and _____, you are husband and wife according to the witness of Christ's Church, in the name of the Father, and of the Son, and of the Holy Spirit. Those whom God has joined together, let no one put asunder. Amen.

NOTES

FREE METHODIST HANDBOOK: MARRIAGE AND WEDDINGS

ABOUT THE AUTHOR

Dr. John Wesley Slider is a Free Methodist pastor in Saint Matthews, Kentucky. John was been married to his wife, Lillian, for more than forty years. She passed away in 2019. John and Lillian had two children – a daughter, Heather; and a son, William, who is married to Tina.

John was licensed to preach in 1975 in the United Methodist Church. He was ordained and Elder, and served as a pastor in that denomination beginning in 1979 and ending with his retirement in 2010. That year he transferred his ordination to the Free Methodist Church and was appointed as a pastor in his new denomination.

John is a graduate of Hanover College where he received a B.A. in history in 1975. He attended Southern Seminary where he received an M.Div. in 1981 and a D.Min. in 1986. He received a Doctor of Divinity in 2019 from the Wesley School of Divinity.

FREE METHODIST HANDBOOK: BAPTISM
VIRTUAL CHURCH RESOURCES
JOHN WESLEY SLIDER

FREE METHODIST HANDBOOK: MARRIAGE AND WEDDINGS
VIRTUAL CHURCH RESOURCES
JOHN WESLEY SLIDER

FREE METHODIST HANDBOOK: A PLAIN ACCOUNT OF CHRISTIAN PERFECTION
VIRTUAL CHURCH RESOURCES
JOHN WESLEY

FREE METHODIST HANDBOOK: HOLINESS TEACHINGS OF B.T. ROBERTS
BENJAMIN TITUS ROBERTS

DR. JOHN WESLEY SLIDER
ADVENT: A LESSON LEARNED
ONE PASTOR'S EXPERIENCE AT STARTING A NEW CHURCH

DR. JOHN WESLEY SLIDER
CIRCLES OF FRIENDS: A LESSON LEARNED

DR. JOHN WESLEY SLIDER
DYS-CONNECTION: A LESSON LEARNED

DR. JOHN WESLEY SLIDER
THE TIMBER LINE: A LESSON LEARNED

SERMONS ON THE FAMILY
William W. Slider
SERMONS BY THE REVEREND DOCTOR WILLIAM W. SLIDER

SERMONS FOR PATRIOTIC SUNDAYS
William W. Slider
SERMONS BY THE REVEREND DOCTOR WILLIAM W. SLIDER

SERMONS ON SELECTED SAYINGS OF JESUS
William W. Slider
SERMONS BY THE REVEREND DOCTOR WILLIAM W. SLIDER

SERMONS FOR THANKSGIVING
William W. Slider
SERMONS BY THE REVEREND DOCTOR WILLIAM W. SLIDER

SERMONS FOR LENT, VOLUME 1
William W. Slider
SERMONS BY THE REVEREND DOCTOR WILLIAM W. SLIDER

NOTES

John Wesley Slider

John Wesley Slider

Made in United States
Orlando, FL
25 June 2024